PRINCES OF THE PLOUGH
The Return of the Heavy Horse

Also by Barry Cockcroft

Hannah in Yorkshire

Sunley's Daughter: The Ways of a Yorkshire Dale

The Dale that Died

I offer my grateful thanks to all those who feature in this book for their generous help and cooperation, particularly Geoffrey Morton. I am also indebted to Alan Harbour for photography and to Julia Suddards for secretarial assistance.

Barry Cockcroft

PRINCES OF THE PLOUGH

The Return of the Heavy Horse

J M Dent & Sons Ltd

London, Melbourne and Toronto

For my mother

First published 1978

© Barry Cockcroft 1978

All Rights Reserved. No part of this publication may be
reproduced, stored in a retrieval system, or transmitted, in
any form or by any means, electronic, mechanical,
photocopying, recording or otherwise, without the prior
permission of J. M. Dent & Sons Ltd.

Printed and bound in Great Britain by
Butler & Tanner Ltd, Frome and London
for J. M. Dent & Sons Ltd
Aldine House, Albemarle Street, London
This book is set in 10 on 11 point Monophoto Plantin

ISBN 0 460 04320 X

British Library Cataloguing in Publication Data

Cockcroft, Barry
　　Princes of the plough.
　　1. Shire horses
　　I. Title
　　636.1'5　　　　　　SF293.S/

ISBN 0–460–04320–X

Contents

I
Origin of the Species

Three decades ago, the Shire horse dominated the landscape of rural Britain. Indeed, it had been for more centuries than written records reveal the absolute monarch of the farmyard—agriculture's principal source of energy, the ultimate workhorse.

Huge, docile and willing, the Shire and kindred breeds of heavy horse obediently plied their rippling power throughout the farming year, equal to any task their masters could set them. Far removed from the glamour and elegance of the hunt, the carriage or the racecourse, they heaved and hauled from first light until sunset.

If strength was their principal asset, then a majestic dignity became their main characteristic. But it was, of course, for their strength that the heavy horse was first brought to these shores. One theory states that the warlords of medieval Britain soon discovered that the creatures indigenous to this country were no match for the giants brought across the seas by the fierce colonizers from Germany and the lowlands of Europe—and, of course, William the Conqueror. They were carefully crossbred into our stock and, encouraged by direct edicts from more than one sovereign, still heavier and even more powerful horses evolved. By the beginning of the fifteenth century, the War Horse—referred to by some early writers as the Great Horse—was ready for battle. It had to be capable of carrying prodigious weights of military hardware. Wrapped in metal plate or chain mail, it was propelled at the enemy carrying a man and armour weighing upwards of a fifth of a ton.

Geoff Morton and Grace

7

There is a school of thought which now maintains that this alliance between the heavy horse and the bold knight is just a romantic vision. They point to the collection of horse armour kept in the Tower of London, which they say is far too small to fit anything as large as a Shire horse. Mr Russell Robinson, Keeper of Armour at the Tower, says that military horses were certainly tall and strong, but nothing more. He does admit that by the early sixteenth century horse armour had become bigger and more elaborate, but he still considers that Shires were never riding horses.

This theory seems to ignore the fact that most things, and certainly men and horses, have evolved upwards. A man considered large in the sixteenth century and before would probably be a seven-stone, sand-in-the-face weakling today; the same must be true of horses. Either way, it is never likely to be proved conclusively. Most will prefer the romantic view, including the Shire Horse Society which proclaims: 'Undoubtedly, the Shire breed was originally developed for military purposes.' So if Richard II really did cry out 'A horse! A horse! My kingdom for a horse', then you can be reasonably sure it was a Shire horse that he meant—or the nearest thing to a Shire that existed at the time.

To the inadequately-armed and poorly-protected peasant pressed into military service by his warrior chief, the sight of a lethal one-ton mixture of muscle and metal thundering down upon him must have been devastating. And yet, when the clang and clamour of war receded, it was the peasant farmer who took over the stewardship of the war horse. He harnessed him to the plough, the heavy cart, fallen trees—to anything beyond the physical capability of humans and lesser animals. They bred him for docility rather than aggressive spirit, for even more strength now that he no longer needed the agility to weave through the hazards of a battlefield with a man on his back. And gradually the ancestors of the Shire spread throughout the land, ousting the ponderous oxen. The breed was reinforced by new blood imported during the seventeenth century from Flemish stock—enormous beasts mainly black in colour. Evidence points to the Fen country being the original centre for the heavy horse, which also makes geographical sense. Farmers in neighbouring counties such as Staffordshire, Leicestershire and Derbyshire quickly became important breeders and between 1755 and 1770 the village of Packenham in Leicestershire enjoyed unaccustomed (and unrepeated) fame. For there stood the Packenham Blind Horse, one of the first great Shire horse stallions. Why, or indeed whether he was blind isn't clear but he certainly sired a stream of highly-prized foals which generally improved the breed. He was succeeded by other prized stallions in the Midlands and to this day the same area is recognized as the natural home of the Shire horse. The principal event of the year for all those involved with the breed is held at the East of England Showground in Peterborough, where the Shire Horse Society has its offices.

Eventually, the major workload of British agriculture was shared by three other breeds of heavy horse: the Clydesdale, the Suffolk and the Percheron. The natural independence of the Scot led to a strain peculiar, in the first instance, to the valley of the Clyde. It is really a Scottish Shire, since it was crossbred from the English strain and developed into a slightly smaller, somewhat less docile beast with characteristic white legs. Regrettably, they proved ideal horses to work in the iron ore mines of Cleveland where the seams were large enough for them to haul tubs full of stone, a dozen at a time, on the rails a thousand feet underground. Countless thousands of Clydesdales were swallowed up over the years by the ninety-seven mines around Guisborough and, compared to their relatives pounding the fields and lanes high above them, led acutely miserable lives. They were even stabled underground and saw daylight just once a year, when the pits closed down for the annual holidays. To see their reaction when they felt the summer grass under their hooves again tore at the emotions, according to one Guisborough blacksmith who often descended the mines to shoe their canker-ridden feet.

'It was marvellous and heartbreaking at one and the same time to watch them. They would gallop around and act like babies, big as they were. And then, after a few blissful days, they were led back down again for the damp and sulphur to eat into their legs, covering them with green slime which would hang down like bunches of grapes.'

The real dandy of the four breeds of heavy horse is unquestionably the Suffolk. Developed in the county of the same name, it is a true aristocrat since the blood line of all true Suffolks leads directly back to one single eighteenth-century horse. It is also the most handsome for the majority are distinguished by a flaxen mane which contrasts, Palamino-style, with their principal chestnut colour. Their heads are more finely sculptured and they frequently sport a pronounced, curving crest. They were bred to a smaller stature than the average Shire, with stubby but well-muscled legs and a longer body to cope with the effort of dragging a plough across the leaden, though extremely fertile, soil typical of the flat lands of East Anglia. It is often referred to as the Suffolk Punch. One would like to think that the sobriquet was added because of the power it applied as it took the first strain of the trace chains.

The one real foreigner among the quartet is the Percheron, a French emigré which became firmly established in this country during the twenties. It has the same military background as its British cousins. Legend says that the Percheron evolved from Arab horses captured by the French from the Saracens in the eighth century. No doubt Percherons charged at the English archers at Agincourt, clattering with the armour of the French nobility. Indeed, they were probably the last of the great war horses for they were drafted in large numbers to serve in the First World War. With strong, shorter legs like the Suffolk, they could drag heavy guns successfully through glutinous Flanders mud which would have swallowed up mules or mechanized transport. They suffered dreadfully as a result, but their ability and remarkable equanimity in terrible conditions so impressed the British heavy horse enthusiasts that they brought them home from the war. They are also very good-looking animals, mainly Ascot grey in colour, which must have also appealed to their new admirers, traditionally more sentimental about horses than the French (who also breed Percherons to eat).

But the supremacy of the English Shire was never seriously challenged. Down the years, he bestrode the fields of his native land like the colossus he certainly is, looming inches taller than the rival breeds and turning the man by his side into a dwarf. From the ground to his massive shoulders, the Shire generally measures a few inches under six feet. If you count in the head and neck it adds another eighteen inches or so. Considering that it weighs around a ton when fully grown, and pounds along on feet as big as soup plates, the Shire is an astonishingly sensitive animal. It shows in the large expressive eyes, and in an un-deviating loyalty to the person who cares for him and orders his working day. He genuinely wants to please at all times.

Bay, black or grey, the Shire has been the closest working companion of the British farmer since the middle ages. In addition to his strength (and records show that two Shires pulling together moved a fifty-ton weight from a standing start), he has the stamina to work long hours and an infinite adaptability. Apart from the obvious tasks in agriculture, the Shire hauled barges up and down the canal system of Britain, pulled trams in the cities, brewers' drays around the pubs, was bred down to become a coach horse and manœuvred railway rolling stock around marshalling yards. The coming of the railways paradoxically led to a dramatic increase in the number of heavy horses. It opened up trading opportunities previously undreamed of, and something was required to move all the new goods piling into and out of the new railway stations. In the early years of this century it is estimated that more than a million-and-a-half Shires and others were sharing the country's major transport burden with the railways.

And then—disaster. The heavy horse collided head-on with the internal combustion engine. Indeed, for all horses outside racing stables the noisy, fume-spewing, new-fangled mode of transport signalled the start of an equestrian Armageddon. Eliminated swiftly from the streets of towns and cities, the horse retrenched in its first and more natural home—the farmyard. Life was tranquil enough through the years between the two world wars, but the threatening rumble of the all-conquering engine grew into a roar during the forties and then burst upon agriculture with devastating results at the end of the war. Almost to a man the farmers of Britain opened their gates to the ugly, smelly but undeniably more efficient tractor and turned out the Shire and his brethren. Obediently and trustingly, they plodded into the knacker's yard and waited for the poleaxe to slam down and turn them into quivering corpses. The thud of a ton of horse-flesh hitting the ground echoed throughout rural Britain and the glue and fertilizer factories never had so much raw material to process. There are no records, but estimates claim the toll reached one hundred thousand a year at its height.

Of course, it made economic if not ecological sense and farmers always seem to live on the brink of financial calamity. It may be easy at this distance to ask whatever became of the bond of affection and loyalty between beast and man, and there was doubtless a lot of soul searching and eventual heartbreak when the decision was made. The carnage was nevertheless appalling, and the Shire horse practically slid into oblivion.

The progress, if not the survival, of any breed of horse depends on careful management. The vital part of any agricultural show lies in the seemingly interminable judging of animals and arable crops by accepted experts. Thus the best strains are picked out, honoured and publicized so that breeders generally are encouraged to take the seed and spread it to improve the whole breed. Just how important one good stallion can be to the future of a species may be judged by the fact that every thoroughbred horse in the world descends from *three* stallions and seventy-eight foundation mares. The Suffolk links directly to just one ancestor, and every other strain of British heavy horse depended entirely, in the late dawn of its evolution, on fewer good brood mares and stallions than would be required to work one medium-sized farm. Clearly, a very slender thread.

Doubtless, the leading pedigree horses did not join the queue at the knacker's yard. After all, enormous sums of money changed hands for the aristocrats of the breed. In the first quarter of this century two thousand guineas was not an unusual price for an outstanding horse, and show champions would fetch twice that. No one in their right minds would turn animals of that calibre into glue, but there was no market for their progeny and most became lonely ornaments. The stud books of each breed, proudly maintained by the various societies since the 1870s, became very sorry volumes indeed.

The prospect of extinction for the Shire was very real in the long term, certainly as a useful, working animal. The lowest ebb came in the fifties and sixties. But a few special men kept faith with the heavy horse, stubbornly refusing to accept what appeared to be an overwhelming argument for total mechanization. Because of them, a noble species had its survival secured and their eccentricity turned out to be inspired foresight.

For the Shire, the Clydesdale, the Suffolk and the Percheron are coming back to where they belong, emerging slowly but triumphantly from the longest and bloodiest battle any war horse had to endure.

2

Violet, Bonny, Beauty, Daisy, Grace—and Geoffrey Morton

Geoffrey Morton completely fulfils everyone's original, picture-book concept of a farmer. Invariably dressed in shapeless tweed, much-abused hat, open-neck shirt hanging out of cord breeches, he is a square-rigged, beetle-browed man with hands like shovels and a craggy face whipped red by constant exposure to the elements. Nothing appears to ruffle him; his speech is slow, measured and richly regional, his mind contrastingly quick and astute.

His farm, isolated on the rolling, windswept plains of east Yorkshire at Holme-on-Spalding Moor is an impressionist painting: squat, stone barns and byres, sepia with age and squared-off to form a cobbled courtyard; steaming middens, sweet-smelling haystacks, sprawling sows with insatiable litters, scratching chickens, ill-tempered geese, friendly dogs; and, above all, Shire horses.

Twenty magnificent beasts roam his fields and do all his work, for Geoff Morton will not tolerate a tractor on his land. To come to Hasholme Carr Farm for the first time when he is ploughing with a four-in-hand against a backdrop of one of the spectacular winter sunsets for which the area is well known, is a stunning experience.

Over the last decade, Geoff, his Shires and his philosophy have so excited the media that he has become far and away the best-known farmer in Britain. Picture editors of national newspapers and magazines despatch their most artistic photographers at regular intervals, and television film crews have

Geoff with his Shires cluttered up his cobbles more times than Geoff can recall. Three full, enormously successful documentaries have been made about his life and horses. The last one, ending with the dramatically difficult birth of a foal, was watched by a rapt audience of many millions and went on to win the Prix Italia (the world's most coveted television award). It was also transmitted, much to Geoff's amusement, on American television—with sub-titles! A sequence of the first documentary, made by Yorkshire Television, was repeated every night for years during the station close-down.

Most people naturally assume Geoff Morton to be an arche-

14

typal countryman, wedded to the land since birth. They are wrong. He was born a 'townie', son of an engineer and seafarer, in the port of Whitby in 1926. When he left school at the age of sixteen, the natural thing to do was to go to sea. His father had, there was a war on and, anyway, job opportunities did not proliferate in Whitby at that time. So he joined the Merchant Navy and for nearly nine years roamed the world, calling at Australia and all the exotic Far East ports, both seaboards of North America, South America, the Caribbean and the Mediterranean. He rose to the position of second mate.

It would also be natural to assume that after so many years and experiences the call of the sea would remain firmly rooted in Geoff Morton for life. Wrong again. The land had first option on his emotions and no amount of seafaring adventures altered that basic fact.

'It's in the blood, I suppose. When I was very young Dad earned his living with horses. I can just remember seeing him working them in the town, going in and out of the stables. My old Uncle John was head horseman on a farm and Dad used to go and work there, too. But he never got a farm of his own and went back to sea.

'It is hard to say when my own involvement with horses started. It's not a thing that really has a beginning—it just seems to have been there all the time. I know I knocked about on farms all the time during my childhood. My Aunt Nancy used to say that I would walk a mile just to ride a hundred yards in a horse and cart. And she was right.'

Geoff believes that most of his forbears worked the land. Indeed, one of them figures in a rural legend which was still being related in the West Riding of Yorkshire not so long ago.

'Aye, that was my great-great-grandfather. He was a cattle drover, a position of some importance in those days, which was round about a hundred and twenty years ago. He owned and worked with a very clever dog, renowned throughout the county for its ability to herd cattle of all kinds. One day he was on the road with a herd when a man came to see him. He wanted to buy the dog and offered a large sum of money. But great-great-grandfather refused point blank, saying no amount of money would persuade him to sell. During the night, the man came back and stole the dog. Next morning, great-great-grandfather and his friends set off in pursuit. For three days they searched but found no trace of dog or thief. So they gave up all hope of ever finding him again and set off on the road with the cattle again.

15

Geoff's son, Andrew, with three grey Shires

'But they hadn't gone very far when the dog turned up behind them—and, furthermore, he had a flock of sheep with him! Oddly enough, they never did find out who owned the sheep— I suppose they didn't try too hard!'

Throughout his own wanderings Geoff never lost interest or contact with agriculture, reading whatever he could to keep himself informed. Back home on leave he met and fell in love with a girl called Lucy, who happened to live at Holme-on-Spalding Moor, slap in the middle of the east Yorkshire farming belt.

16

'The war was over so I decided to come ashore for good and get married. It seemed a natural thing to turn to the land. And quite a few smallholdings came up for rent around that time in the Holme-on-Spalding Moor district, so we put in for one. It had about ten acres of ploughing land and it was possible to make a living off a small spread like that then, growing cash crops like sugar beet, carrots, barley and wheat. You couldn't make a start on a place so small now, even if you could find one, because the returns would be too low. Anyway, smallholdings by and large don't exist any more because they have all either been built on or absorbed into bigger farms.

'With being away at sea I had missed seeing the early part of the sweeping mechanization that happened on the land. The last farm I'd had any experience of was run with horses, so I came back still thinking of horses. It never occurred to me at first that there was a choice. Everyone thinks that I did make a deliberate choice to use horses instead of tractors, but I looked at it from the other side. I've always felt that the question "why horses instead of tractors" was really the wrong one. Horses have always seemed the proper thing, the logical thing to me, so I think the right question should be "why tractors instead of horses".

'Anyway, at first I couldn't afford anything of my own, horse or tractor. I had to work for a big farmer on a neighbouring spread during the day and buckle to on my own place at nights and weekends. My employer still had a pair of Shire horses then which weren't doing a great deal of work, so he allowed me to use them at weekends. It was good for them as well as handy for me because they needed work to keep fit. That arrangement carried on for a while until I managed to acquire more land which meant I had to give up working for someone else.'

So, with very few acres but a lot of courage, Geoff and his bride broke free and faced up to the rigours and risks of independent farming. They agreed that their first major capital expenditure item should be—a Shire horse. There were still a few to be found around the area and the time was spring, traditionally the season for farm sales. Geoff trailed round looking for the right horse, making the odd, unsuccessful bid. And then a sale was announced with four horses listed among the livestock.

'One of them was a very fine animal, a nine-year-old grey Shire mare called Violet. I knew as soon as I saw her that she was the one for me and I did well to get her. We still have Violet. She's just over thirty years old now and she doesn't do much,

Andrew (riding) and Geoff
bring in the harvest

but she is welcome to stay as long as she doesn't become ill
and continually in pain. Most Shire horses don't get a chance
to live out their full lifespan because they usually develop
serious trouble in their feet and legs and have to be put down.
But Violet's legs are still sound, and she occasionally does the
odd job which seems to keep her in better shape.'

Violet obviously holds a special place in the affections of
Geoff Morton—and farmers, particularly Yorkshire farmers,
are anything but sentimental about animals (they simply can't
afford to be). But then, she has given him twenty years of honest
toil, and at the same time been an outstanding brood mare. Two
years ago, one of her grand-daughters gave birth to a grey filly
foal. Four generations of Shire horse on the same farm, and
all grey, is more than just unusual. Violet and her progeny form
the main prop in the argument Geoff has been conducting now
for two decades with other farmers and people concerned with
agriculture, which is being debated more and more these days:
the case of the tractor versus the horse.

Geoff Morton presents his brief with the relaxed assurance
of a man who knows that the evidence is beginning to weigh
heavily in his favour.

'The basic thing is that horses are breeding their own
replacements all the time. All you need is a stock of mares and
the cycle is self-perpetuating. Over the years I think I have
bought five horses and sold three times that number. These

days a good filly foal can go for between three to five hundred guineas, a colt around two hundred, a good four-year-old mare in foal might be worth a thousand or more; and prices are going up all the time. I was lucky in starting my stock when horses were considered redundant and prices were consequently low.

'Now breeding does not interrupt the work flow because a mare can keep going right up to foaling—it's better for her, in fact. I generally give them about a week off after the birth. There is a gap of about two years before the foals are ready for the bigger tasks but they are generally able to do a bit of light work.

'If you use a tractor, you first of all have to find two or three thousand pounds—or even more, these days—to buy it. And who knows how much they will be next year. Then you have to go out and make some money with it to pay for the oil and rubber that it uses and for the mechanic who fixes it when it goes wrong. Not only does it not reproduce itself, after about five or six years, it's finished—just scrap value. But a horse goes on increasing in value until it is seven years old and holds its price for quite a few more years after that. And it is always worth something, however old it is.

'Now a lot of people say that it must cost a great deal to feed twenty horses, but the farm is self-supporting. In the past few years our major source of income—the main cash crop, you might say—has been pigs. About seven hundred a year we have been breeding. So nearly all the produce of the farm, apart from

Left: Geoff, Andrew, Shire and cart

Right: Hasholm Carr Farm

an acreage of potatoes, has been fed to the pigs and the horses. The system works out very well in more ways than one. To begin with, on tractor-powered farms they are striving to grow as much corn as possible, but there is a limit to the amount most land will yield continually. You are forced to put in what are called break crops—oats, root crops or grass. That has created real problems for ordinary farms because the returns are not good. But on this farm it's ideal. The horses eat the break crops and in turn provide manure to help grow the corn in the following year.

'So, with horses you are taking money out of one pocket and putting it back in the other—with a bit of interest, if you are lucky. This means you are insulated from economic conditions like rising oil prices and all the other things that inflation brings. There is even a measure of protection against Governments chopping and changing their agricultural policies. But most important of all, as far as finance is concerned, you are not at the mercy of machinery manufacturers and Arab oil sheikhs.'

But Geoff's belief in the benefits of horsepower goes far deeper than mere economics and no one should assume that he runs his farm today as a result of a lucky mixture of accident, foresight, eccentricity and native shrewdness. Much as he loves his horses, they are only part of a concept which transcends annual balance sheets, trying to judge markets or weather or any of the other day-to-day details of a farmer's life.

Now ecology is a very fashionable subject and the multitudinous threats to the very nature of this planet engage many of the finest brains in the world. They set in the Halls of Academe and worry both themselves and every other responsible person about the imbalances created by what people are pleased to call the dynamic progress of man. With their finely-tuned minds and computers as big as haystacks, they view the problems on a global scale. Geoff Morton's formal education ended before he began to shave and he modestly claims that ecology is a subject 'almost too big for peasants like me'. But he admits to being gravely concerned about the disturbing things he sees happening around him, and since he is both keenly observant and a natural philosopher, and daily engaged in the very area where some of the most immediately dangerous abuses against nature are being committed—namely, agriculture—he has become a grassroots ecologist in every sense of the word. His views and conclusions are as valid as anyone's, and in his own, small way he is doing his responsible best to redress the balance on his own land and give an example to others.

Geoff is not a proclaimer of impending doom, but he does believe that agriculture should reorganize sensibly back to a proper, harmonious partnership with nature.

'Nature is a very strong force and would fight back against the bad things we are doing given any help at all. Otherwise we will be made to return to what I feel is a more balanced, better and natural way of farming. I know this may be an unpopular view to hold, but it will have to come whether we like it or not. Is it not better to recognize this and go comfortably along with it rather than have it forced on us in the end?

'Advanced technology seemed such a marvellous thing, particularly when it first arrived on the farm. It made life so much

Geoff brings in his horses to start the day's work

21

Geoff and friends   easier for the farmer and the new and powerful chemicals swept away all kinds of problems in no time at all. They appeared to be the answer to everything. Trouble is that invariably they left behind an even greater difficulty than the problem they got rid of.

'Take the current trouble with wild oats. All corn growers now are plagued with wild oats—they have exploded all over the country. No doubt this is partly due to the use of combine harvesters. The corn is cut at a later stage when the wild oats have had time to shed their seed. Now if you use a binder in the old way any wild oats are cut and taken off the field largely before the seeds have had a chance to drop. But the main reason to my mind can be found in all the weed killers that we farmers used twenty years ago to get rid of charlock and fat hen and other troublesome wild plants. It seemed so amazing at the time but it created a vacuum and nature just will not have that. She will fill it, and unfortunately she filled it with wild oats which are worse than charlock and fat hen.

22

Geoff with his son Andrew

'And then we have insecticides which you can apply to your sugar beet or mangle crops if they are attacked by the black fly. They certainly do a wonderful job of exterminating black fly, but they also wipe out ladybirds and all the other harmless insects that prey upon the black fly as nature intended. Whereas in the past we seemed to get a bad attack of the black fly maybe every four or five years, nowadays we have a bad attack every year and we have to use the spray every year.

'The only people who have gained anything out of all this are the people who make the sprays. I think we would be far better off accepting the black fly every four or five years and let the ladybirds take care of them during the years in between.'

Geoff has many more alarming examples of direct conflicts between nature and commercial technology to recount. Because they are founded upon years of personal experience and intelligent observation they chill the soul far more than the pronouncements of academics who never get mud on their boots. And so many of the solutions lead back directly to the horse.

23

'With horses, nature imposes the balance. You cannot take out more than you put in. There is more harmony than with a highly-mechanized system where you are increasingly putting a lot more into the land—dangerous things—than you are getting out as an end product. Of course, the work has to be spread out more if you use horses. You cannot allow it to pile up into peaks quite as much. But on the other hand you can keep on working with horses when the weather forces you to quit with a tractor and put it back in the shed. Particularly when you are trying to get the ploughing done in winter.'

Geoff's major argument against the tractor concerns land compaction which he has been doggedly expounding for many years and which has now become widely accepted. When a horse puts a hoof down it compresses a small area of soil as it pulls and then strides over the rest. Tractors continually pound our arable land and when it is wet—and most ploughing is done in the winter months—they slide and smear the soil with disastrous consequences in many cases.

'You see, the whole soil structure is destroyed by the continual use of tractors in the wrong conditions. The air channels are damaged, roots cannot get through and neither can moisture, which leds to drainage problems. Consequently you get trouble with trace elements. So what do you have to do— why, use more sprays and more chemicals to counteract the trouble. Farmers are being forced on to roundabouts that they cannot get off and it is alarming to watch the extremes to which they are driven.

'Now you have to use medicines for the land just as you have to use them for yourself. But there is a world of difference between medicine and drug addiction.

'And I'm sad to say that too much of this nation's agricultural land is addicted to drugs.'

Among the many chemical additives used by farmers throughout Britain, Geoff is particularly concerned about nitrogen. He says that a large proportion of agricultural dressings are nitrogen based, and he believes that a very substantial residue of that is not going into the plants, but into our drinking water.

'When you start using nitrogen to get an extra yield you often have to put more and more on to maintain that yield every year. But the stuff is turning into nitrates and filtering into the drainage water. Then it goes into the ground water and comes out at the bore holes. Round this part of the East Riding of Yorkshire most of the drinking water comes from bore holes in the

24

chalk. They had to shut down one supply because it became unsafe for children. There is no doubt that many water authorities are extremely worried about the nitrate content in their supplies, but there isn't much they can do about it, as far as I can tell. It isn't scientifically possible to prove where all the nitrogen is coming from so they cannot bring court actions against the individuals responsible. But I have no doubt at all that the nitrate levels in the ground water have risen in the same proportions and over the same time scale as the amount of nitrogen dressings used on agricultural land.

'I'm not exactly a pensioner yet, but I can remember the time when we didn't have any pesticides, insecticides and sprays and we seemed to get through the farming year all right. And I am sure that we shall have to give up chemicals in the end if we want a country that is fit to live in—or even possible to live in. I think that we are only just beginning to feel the bad effects of DDT and all the other, even more powerful forms of chemical aids we have been, and are using. I'm afraid that our children, and even their children will not think very well of us for the harm we have done to the land we shall pass on to them. It will take that long for some of the consequences to show.

'I think it is time we stopped—now.'

3

A New Breed—of Horse and Man

In the uncompromising company of the heavy horse society, Charles Pinney would seem at first glance to be totally out of place. As he mingles with the elders at the Peterborough Show in spring or the Midlands Shire Foal Show in autumn—the two great annual gatherings of the clans—one could easily assume he had strayed from the paddock at Ascot.

The average heavy horse enthusiast is a stern and lumpy middle-aged man with the build of a small barn door and a keen disregard for sartorial splendour, deliberate of movement and richly accented in speech. By comparison, Charles Pinney is a mere stripling—a youth in his middle twenties—and dresses his slim form in clothes which were clearly made to fit him. He also smiles a lot and his free-flowing speech would meet the full approval of the BBC. And yet . . . he moves among his seniors with an unusual authority. Men like Geoff Morton and the other giants of the brethren greet him with much enthusiasm and, would you believe, marked respect. Heavy horse men are supposed to serve half a lifetime to their craft before admittance is granted to the inner councils. Just over six years ago, Charles Pinney's knowledge of horse power was largely restricted to motor cycles, but today his position among the men who have pivoted their lives around the heavy horse for longer than he has lived is not only remarkable—it is unique. He achieved it by a mixture of the reckless confidence of youth and an entrepreneurial ability to spot an opportunity and exploit it.

Charles Pinney was destined for agriculture from birth and

was given a racing start. He took over a 250-acre family farm
in Bettiscombe, Bridport, among the lush acres of Dorset, at
the unusually early age of twenty. It is not an easy farm despite
its generous size and its location amid what northern hill
farmers would call the soft underbelly of this nation's farming
land.

'Only about a hundred acres are really any good,' says
Charles. 'The rest comprises rough grazing and steep hillside
with a lot of heavy clay. Basically, I raise corn, beef and sheep.'

Horses played no part in his early life. Indeed, it was exclusively geared to the internal combustion engine. Tractors on
the farm and motor cycles for pleasure—Charles's youth was
largely spent ploughing around those heavy hillsides at
scramble events, hurling his machine through mudbaths and
leaping over obstacles. The lure of horseriding passed him by.
He started his farming career with two old tractors and seemed
the least likely candidate in British agriculture to consider seriously whether there might be some advantage to be gained by
replacing them with horses. But he did, and the entire movement gained as a result.

'Years ago my family had dealt with a heavy horse breeder
at Blandford so I got in touch with him. He was still in business

Geoff Norton and Charles Pinney debate the quality of the Ardennes breed

and I bought a Percheron gelding from him for £250—round about sixteen three hands. It was called Horatio and I had no idea how to handle the thing. So I went round all the local ancients and asked them for advice. At first I used him just to carry the milk up to the end of the drive for collection.

'There were one or two hairy moments in the beginning because of my ignorance at handling him. I would hitch him incorrectly and he would object strenuously, scattering off and distributing implements thinly all round the field.

'Eventually I learned and found that Horatio was ideal for all the short carrying jobs, taking the feed up to the cows on the hillsides, going through orchards and into low buildings where an ordinary tractor could not possibly reach. All that kind of stop–start haulage work is much better done with a horse because you don't have to keep clambering on and off its back and it won't tip over. To get the same kind of efficiency on my

28

farm I would have had to spend six or seven thousand pounds on a four-wheel-drive tractor.

'Nevertheless, buying a horse was just a pleasant notion at the outset, I suppose. But I was amazed that one could justify one's romantic vision with hard economics. It turned out to be a completely viable proposition, quite apart from the ecological considerations like soil pannage caused by tractors.'

Charles had two happy and useful years with Horatio when disaster struck. One day, the poor beast dropped dead. Enough, you might think, to put most people off horses for good, but Charles went back to the same dealer and acquired two more heavy horses.

'I bought whatever was available and workable. I wasn't concerned about breed and pedigree at the time. They turned out to be Shire cross. Eventually I built up to six horses and got rid of the two tractors. But then I ran into a problem when I wanted to increase my stock yet again. It became clear to me, after several visits to the main auction sales, that the heavy horses coming on to the market were either too large or too expensive to be economically justifiable.

'I began to find them unsatisfactory for working on the hillsides. Their height was wrong; if you like, they were top heavy and their draught angle was much too high, which meant they were tending to lift rather than pull implements. You need a horse to be between fifteen and sixteen hands for my kind of work, but most of the breeders seemed to be aiming at between seventeen and eighteen hands.

'It was quite a problem—I just couldn't get one to suit me.'

And it was at this point in 1975 that Charles Pinney took, in one giant stride, his place among the genuine pioneers of the heavy horse fraternity. What he did was part accidental, seemingly impossible and wholly impertinent, in that older and more experienced men would have dismissed his scheme out of hand as a prime example of the crassness of youth. Yet it was beautifully simple.

'I just got hold of a book about French breeds of heavy horse and flipped through until I found the nicest looking dumpy, short animal. It turned out to be an Ardennes, so I decided that was the one for me. Apart from any other consideration, it seemed such a good idea to try another breed.'

Now there were no Ardennes horses in Britain at the time, as far as anyone knew. And the problems of moving any kind of animal from one country to another—particularly if the receiving country is Britain—are enormous. The very real fear of passing disease in this way has lead to a high wall of restrictions. But Charles breezed blithely ahead and wrote to the French Ministry of Agriculture and the breed society announcing his intention of one day setting up an Ardennes stud in Britain, and could they kindly and quickly assist him to find a mare of the right kind and at the right price to get him started. Of course, anyone could have told him that bureaucracy across the channel makes the kind we have to suffer in Britain appear amazingly efficient, and ridiculously benevolent. But if they did, he took no notice.

'The French authorities were fantastic, marvellous! They fixed up all the arrangements for me to visit various studs and even went round with me because my French isn't terribly good. We toured a lot of places in the Ardennes area, which runs down the border with Belgium. And most of them turned out to be mares because they don't go in for geldings at all. They cut off their heads instead and eat them.

'The heavy horse is still used quite a lot on small French farms, but most Ardennes are bred for meat now, which is

A close up examination

something of a shame. One farm we went to had ninety of them running around like beef cattle. None of them worked—they just rounded them up twice a year and the fat ones were picked out and sent to the butcher.

'The advantage they do gain, however, is that a horse does not depreciate much because when it has finished its working life it can still be sold for meat.

'In fact the French are pretty well organized with their horses and all their pedigree stock is registered, like cars in this country, to indicate their age. Their names have to start with the year's letter, G or H or whatever it might be.

'Anyway my trip to France ended up at this top stud farm and I looked around in despair because they appeared far too expensive for my pocket. Indeed, the woman who ran it was in the habit of supplying champions to their national stud. But I pointed one out, said I would like that and asked how much. They said a thousand pounds. I told them that was no good, not an economical proposition and they mustn't think I was a lunatic American. And the owner was so taken with the idea of her horses being exported to Britain that she let me have two mares—both in foal—at a very reasonable price. In fact, I got them back to this country for seven and eight hundred pounds each. Which is not bad when compared with two thousand quid for a two-year-old Shire mare in foal.

'I had no real problems with the paperwork. The French fixed it all up for me at no cost to myself, including the provision of International Veterinary Certificates for our Ministry people. They run an organization dealing solely with the export of animals. The only hiccup in a remarkably smooth operation came when I trotted into the customs shed in Calais with my two mares. They held me up for eighteen hours. Although I had all the right bits of paper, I didn't have a bit of paper which *said* I had all the right bits of paper!'

Charles arrived triumphantly back with his two French mares—Goget and Hotain—at Home Farm in May 1975, and set about founding Bettiscombe Cart Horses, which is clearly doing well. Charles has been a farmer long enough now to display the classic reluctance of that ilk to admit to prosperity, and turns a neat phrase to get round any close questioning about the subject. He says he is not losing money faster than any other farmer in his particular area! But about his Ardennes mares he can be as lyrical as a poet.

'They have fulfilled my wildest dreams, really. They are enormously strong but extremely compact and most important

31

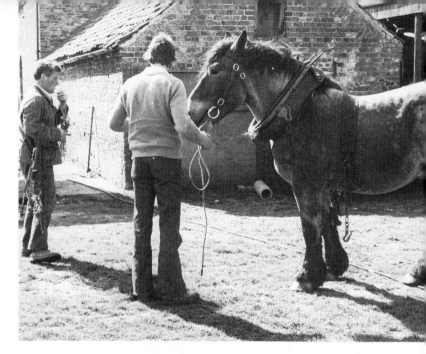

32

Charles Pinney struggling to control his Ardennes stallion prior to a mating

of all—much more docile than any other breed I know about. Docility is a major advantage because if you are to make a realistic job of farming with horses you have to work with animals that will not only do their job but allow you to get on with yours. Teamwork is essential. If you are using a mowing machine, a binder or a plough you want the horse to get on with the pulling whilst you deal with the machinery side of it. You just cannot afford to have stroppy and difficult beasts.

'And then the Ardennes is structurally exactly right for what I want. They have a short back, with a very deep and broad chest so that internal organs have plenty of room to work, huge joints which wear very well and good, hard black feet which don't tend to split and therefore minimize shoeing. In fact, if you didn't do road work with an Ardennes you wouldn't need to shoe it at all.'

Charles' enthusiasm for the Ardennes is already proving infectious. Even Geoff Morton, champion of the Shire, readily admits to a long-standing admiration for the French breed.

'I knew about the Ardennes many years ago and thought they were a good proposition. They still are. But it was easier to work with what there was when I was starting, and in those days France was a lot further away. But if we hadn't been so lucky in being able to start with a good strain of Shire I might very well have looked abroad.'

33

Charles and Geoff met when the younger man was in his
formative days with heavy horses, and the two obviously liked
each other from the start. Charles readily acknowledges a debt
of gratitude to Geoff for a lot of help and advice when he needed
it most and the two keep in regular contact. Indeed, the pupil
may eventually influence the master because Geoff has been
down to Dorset to inspect the Ardennes.

'He seemed to be very impressed,' Charles declares proudly.
'And he says he may even come with me on my next visit to
France. You see, I want a stallion now—and another mare or
two, if I can afford it—so that I can found the first Ardennes
stud in this country, and really get the breed established. It will
be very reassuring for me to have Geoff along because he knows
as much about heavy horses as anyone. He will stop me buying
one with a leg missing, or something! And he may even invest
himself. There was a time, round about a hundred and fifty
years ago, when Ardennes stallions were imported to Britain
in substantial numbers to improve the Shire. Even the
Ardennes stallion has a stable temperament which means you
can also work him, within reason. That is a prime consideration
these days when there is a dearth of skilled horsemen.'

All the day-to-day motive power at Home Farm is supplied
by horses, and Charles handles them without hired hands. His
sole help, except at the busiest times, comes from his wife. At
one stage he built up to a dozen horses by investing in a small
Shire stallion and putting him to his mares. But he has sold
off most of the colts in order to raise the cash to finance his
investment in the French breed. Naturally he still has his two
Ardennes mares and one foal—the other, unfortunately, died
from a kidney ailment. The elder of the two mares was put to
the Shire stallion because Charles wanted to try one cross and,
anyway, there was no stallion of the same breed around. But
he left the other one empty because she is young, needs the
breathing space and will be ready for an Ardennes stallion when
he manages to acquire one.

Although the tractor has been banished from his domain,
Charles does have to seek aid from mechanical sources at crucial
times of the year, such as haymaking and harvest when there
is always pressure from time and weather. He hires the services
of contractors with specialized machinery. At the moment, it
is not possible to hire enough experienced men to take out sufficient teams of horses to get the work done. Typically, Charles
has set about solving this problem in the same enterprising and
fearless way which sent him across the channel. When he gets

35

an idea he does not hang about, and he goes straight to the top.

'Now I was lucky when I started out with horses because I had access to a few local people with experience and I eventually met people like Geoff Morton and Nick Rayner, who runs a Shire stud in the New Forest. But there were occasions when I was absolutely stuck on my own in real trouble, no idea what to do and no one to turn to. Obviously there is an infinite number of people in this country who have worked with horses in the past but they are not always forthcoming about explaining the finer points. Sometimes it is a case of grabbing them by the jacket and shaking them until the information falls out.

'There are lots of people who are mad keen to work with horses again—you should see the letters I get—so a few of us in the west country came together and started a small society with a view to exchanging information and, more important, to speaking with a united voice trying to bully people into making machinery and harness again, which are always a headache to find. It's called the Western Counties Heavy Horse Society and I became vice-chairman. In 1975 I went along to Smith-

field, trundled up to the Agricultural Training Board stand and had a heart-to-heart talk with an official. I told him about our ninety members, thirty of whom had horses and about a dozen badly needing advice and assistance. Could the Board help? He said it could and together we set about organizing a course. The Board arranged for everybody to come, paid the students and gave them travel allowances and so on. They made me the instructor, gave me a fee and also pay for the facilities I provide. The first dozen or so who have joined the course are very serious about it. They are all youngish or early middle-aged farmers and market gardeners who are beginning, or thinking of using horses again. It looks like expanding because we have had a lot of good publicity. The *Farmers' Weekly* came and did an article about it and we have been on television which has led to applications from all over the country.'

The progress of Charles Pinney, from total novice to heavy horse instructor and prospective founder of a nationally exclusive stud in six short years, is probably unparalleled in this enclosed society. He is completely modest about his achieve-

Charles Pinney demonstrates the efficiency of the Ardennes

ments and recognizes that he still has much to accomplish and that there are many risks in the business of horse breeding.

'Of course it would be nice to do nothing but own a stud farm. But I am not going to kid myself that there is a living in breeding horses. I think I am on to a worthwhile thing with the Ardennes. Quite apart from the advantages they carry, they are so much more of an economic proposition than the Shire. If I sold all my existing horses I would probably be able to buy one good pedigree Shire mare, which is putting an awful lot of eggs into one basket. Now I expect to pay around a thousand pounds for a first-class Ardennes stallion, which is a quarter of the price I would have to fork out for a Shire stallion of the same quality.

'I don't suppose I will ever become just a horse dealer, however well the stud may go. For it to be meaningful and useful to the heavy horse cause in general I think I should carry on with the corn, beef and sheep at the same time, so I can show that I'm farming with them in a viable way.

'Putting the entire thing in a genuine, up-to-date, economical agricultural context is my aim.'

4
Birth and Afterbirth

The vast majority of British farms, whether large, medium or small, could be worked efficiently and profitably today by the heavy horse—without any aid from the tractor.

So asserts Geoff Morton, who may be the high priest of the movement (a title more thrust upon him than sought) but who can present very convincing evidence to support the theory—and more and more British farmers are beginning to believe him. There is a distinctly discernible and steadily growing trend back to classic horse power throughout the country. Geoff says there seem to be three main categories among the converted.

'There are those who never did get rid of all their horses when the tractor arrived but kept the odd one or two because they liked to have them about the place and wanted to show them. There are others who belong to farming families with a long association with horses in the past so advice, and sometimes a bit of machinery and harness, was readily available. And then there are those who have no knowledge or experience at all, who are starting up as best they can. I get a tremendous amount of mail from the novice category. They write pleading for permission to come to my farm and stay for periods ranging from a month upwards so that they can learn how to handle Shires. Some are only sixteen or seventeen years old. Among the typical cases was a man who had been market gardening on about thirty acres in Hampshire and then sold out for a good price to developers. He wanted to start a beef and sheep farm with a certain amount of cultivation and do it all with horses.

Portrait of a square-rigged man

Another, more unusual instance was a chap in his thirties over from South Africa who wanted to live and work at my farm for two years! I just cannot help anyone to that extent because it would mean people living in. We don't have the accommodation for them and even if we had, it would mean the womenfolk would have to be around all the time.'

And Geoff's womenfolk—his wife, Lucy, and daughter, Janet, would not take kindly to that. They are both absorbed in careers of their own—as school teachers. For a busy and successful farmer, Geoff is as helpful as he possibly can be to anxious, would-be beginners but can be of more practical use to people like Charles Pinney, who go in at the deep end and show determination and initiative.

'Basically, I suppose I am not much in favour of training schemes. I have always been a great believer in that old Yorkshire adage, "Fend for thissen", but I recognize that will not do any more if we are going to have people working with horses

40

again on a serious scale. It was perfectly all right in the old days when there were plenty of farms using horses and plenty of jobs going. You could just grow into the job like my two sons have done. I remember Mark when he was eight years old saying that he knew a lot about horses but then he ought to because he had spent all his life with them!

'Now I admit we need a well-run training scheme organized on a national basis. Private individuals like me cannot possibly cope with the job.'

Apparently, the biggest swing back to horses is in the south of England. But however great the desire to change—even if every farmer in the land tried overnight to trade in his tractor for seventeen-and-a-half hands of horseflesh—it will be painfully slow and gradual. To begin with, there are not enough horses of any kind, and certainly not of the right kind. There was once a beautifully-balanced breeding system in Britain, fashioned over the centuries, which was totally wrecked during the great massacre of the fifties. Geoff Morton likens it to a pyramid, with the bottom layers representing the thousands of ordinary, non-pedigree animals shouldering the main burden of work. The peak represented the very best horses that won the championships at the Royal Show. And the top horses were not pampered ornaments like some of the rosette-laden beasts today. They had to be tough working animals, obliged to do their share in the fields in between parading round show-rings, with manes plaited and decked out in fancy ribbons.

'And they were used to keep the standards reasonably high. Their seed was spread right throughout the pyramid and if there was anything wrong with one of them, say from the temperament point of view, we all soon found out and that strain wasn't used any more. But that working base was largely eliminated and we have since tended to breed horses just for the sake of showing. Only the looks mattered and the entire breed lost out on good temperament, which is vital in a working horse, as a result.

'Without wishing to dramatize it, I suppose that the heavy horse was really in danger of extinction as a working animal. It is the same with dogs and cattle as well—if you start breeding exclusively for show points you inevitably lose the practical, working strains. There are collies which are so highly bred to make them very narrow between the eyes that there is no room for any brains. They are useless! Similarly, a few years back they bred Ayrshire cattle for very fancy udders and nearly spoiled them as good dairy animals.

41

'Unfortunately, as far as the Shire horse is concerned the traditional qualities were entirely bred out of some strains. Not all of them by any means, but several are not as good as they should be from the point of view of docility.

'So the first hurdle for any would-be heavy horse owner is—find a good, unspoiled animal. Or two—or three! You cannot work a farm of viable size with just one. The capital outlay could be high of course. A thousand pounds is a low price for a proven horse.'

Geoff Morton does not come down too heavily in favour of the Shire, though. He says there are splendid horses in all the breeds and indicates that the best course of action is to seek your horse among the most popular breed in the area you intend to farm.

'I suppose if I had lived in Cambridge I might well have started and stayed with Percherons; or Suffolks if it had been the eastern counties; or Clydesdales if my place had been further north. It just happened that Shires were the most common in the part of Yorkshire where I set up shop, so it was that much easier to begin with them and keep on breeding. They are perhaps the biggest of the heavy horses, easy to break, wear well and keep going on the job. Pretty good at reproducing themselves too—in fact, a useful horse all round.'

The development and skilled supervision of successful breeding is central to the whole business of working with horses. The initial capital outlay can eventually be recouped over and over again if the owner has a little good fortune. Geoff Morton, with a vast fund of experience, says the first thing you need is faith.

'You have to show faith in your horses and faith in yourself. If you have, it is relatively easy. It was even easier in the old days when there were a great number of stallion hiring societies covering most of the country. The small farmers with just a few mares between them could club together and hire the services of a high-class stallion which they would never have been able to afford individually. The number of Shire Horse Societies declined along with the horse population, but there are still eight very active survivors. We have a good one in Yorkshire and we spend a lot of time and thought in selecting the right kind of stallion to hire for the breeding season from March through to July. He will be picked out by a committee and terms negotiated months before the season starts.

'A mare that has just had a foal is the easiest to put in foal again. She should be covered about the eighth or ninth day after

The various stages
of serving Geoff's
Ardennes mare with
Charles' Ardennes
stallion

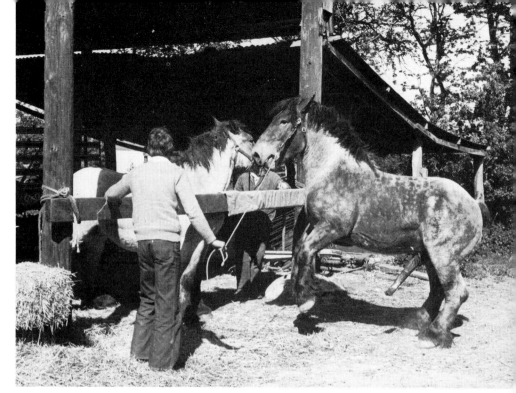

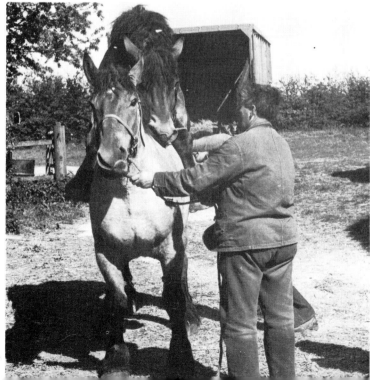

Both men working in the fields with the two horses immediately after the coupling—a remarkable demonstration of the equanimity of the breed. A Shire stallion would have gone mad

the birth and there will be higher than 75 per cent chance. With maiden mares and those which were barren or rested the previous year, the only thing to do is start at the beginning of the season and try them once a week with a stallion until they are ready to accept him.

'It can be a dodgy business. We put up a good, strong bar of wood between two gate posts and bring the stallion up to one side and the mare up to the other. The bar is for the protection of both the stallion and his groom because if the mare is not in season she will most likely kick very savagely to indicate she wishes to have nothing to do with him. But if she sniffs and noses up to him and eventually swings sideways round to the bar we know she is ready and we can safely bring the stallion round to her side. We usually try again the following week because if they are still in season she is obviously not in foal, and again after three weeks, and again until the stallion returns to his owner.'

Clearly, the dairy farmer—with the quick, relatively sure and infinitely simpler method of artificial insemination—has an enormous advantage over the horse breeder when it comes to propagation. It does not stop there—the next harrowing experience can easily be the actual foaling, always providing the animal is pregnant.

Geoff knows better than most the dangers and anxieties associated with that moment. The most memorable sequence in the award-winning Thames Television documentary, which riveted audiences on several continents, was an agonizingly difficult foaling in his stables. The vet had to be called out in the middle of the night and Geoff's image as a kindly and feeling person gained enormously as he soothed, comforted and talked to the distressed mare whilst waiting for help to arrive.

'You just never know with a mare. Unlike most animals they don't always foal near to the date you predict. It can happen a month early or a month late. There is very little to see beforehand. Right at the point of birth some will be very calm, others will become very uneasy. I like to box them for about a fortnight before foaling, but just about the only indication that she is close is wax forming on the end of her teats. Then you can be reasonably sure there will be a foal within forty-eight hours, and usually a much shorter time than that. But she can look perfectly all right and five minutes later you can have a foal born and on its feet. It's all over very quickly if there isn't any trouble. I like to be with mares when that is happening to them, but I've known times when I've just nipped back to the house for a few minutes to have a cuppa and returned to find it all over.

'Mares are, by and large, fairly free from foaling problems. But if you do get trouble then it's usually very bad trouble and if you don't spot it and act very quickly you will have a dead foal, and maybe a dead mare as well, on your hands. That very nearly happened when the television crew filmed Grace giving birth. In a normal foaling the first thing you see are the front feet appearing, and if the nose follows you know things are going well. But poor Grace wasn't getting on with it as she should have been and when I put my hand inside I could feel the foal's head was tucked under with its nose back in towards its chest. But I couldn't reach to get it turned round the right way, so I got the vet to come.

'In any case, that sort of operation can be very risky. If you are trying to put things right inside and the mare puts a really big contraction on—and you have to feel them to know just how powerful they are—they can easily break a man's arm. And if Grace had gone on pushing and pushing with her foal in that position something would have had to give. She would have torn herself terribly and probably broken the foal's neck. All kinds of dreadful things can happen if you don't get on to these things in time, and if necessary, send for professional help.

'Fortunately, Grace delivered her foal safely, but I am sure that if I had delayed getting down to finding out what was wrong by another hour, there would have been bad trouble. She had a colt. We called him Thames and people who watched the programme have turned up at the farm in their dozens to find out how he is getting along.'

There is always a curious little ceremony on the Morton farm after the birth of a foal. The cleansing or afterbirth is taken out and placed on a holly bush or a thorn tree—an act which has echoes of the superstitions of civilizations long gone. Geoff, as usual, knows all about the origins.

'You have to understand that the horse was a sacred animal to all the Nordic peoples thousands of years back. Man in northern Europe has been dependent on horses for as far back as we can find out anything about him at all. So it's not surprising that a great body of superstition with a religious basis grew up around the horse. I suppose Christianity stamped out most of that, but there are remnants of the old customs still lingering about here and there. Putting out the cleansing on holly or thorn is a northern thing, and we still do it on this farm. It doesn't do any harm and who knows—it maybe brings us a bit of good luck and fertility for the mares during the next year.'

5

Multi-Horse Power

Once you are successfully through the lottery of mating, and the nerve-wracking time of maternity is over with the afterbirth hanging from a bush and the young foal romping unsteadily in a quiet field, comes the easy part—breaking and training. Well, Geoff Morton finds this part of the development of a heavy horse comparatively restful. But you have to wait for two years before a foal can start contributing to the working pattern of a farm.

'It won't cost much as it grows up, though. Young horses will do very well on grass for a large part of the year since they are not using their energy in harness, and get along nicely on not very much corn during the winter. The traditional time to break a new horse into work is just after one of your mares has foaled. She will work half a day and the other half will suckle her foal. The young horse can take her place when she is suckling, starting with a little bit of harrowing or other light work. By winter when he is coming up to three he will normally be capable of quite a bit of ploughing, and by the time he is four he should start a full working day.

'Training is not too difficult, if you are reasonably fortunate. Horses are friendly creatures and are generally anxious to please you, but the big difficulty is getting them to understand just what will please you. They are not clever animals but they do have a long and an excellent memory. It's all a matter of persuading them to do the right thing first time. Then they will go on doing it the right way from then on. But if you let them

Geoff with his two Ardennes mares at Holme-on-Spalding Moor

do the wrong thing the first time it will take you a long, long time to correct it.

'To begin with we generally put on girths and side reins and fit a breaking bit in their mouth, and turn them loose in the foal yard to let them help themselves for about a fortnight. After that we spend half an hour driving them about on a pair of long reins, hoping for the best. And the best is what you will get with a bit of luck. But you must work them gently and not overdo things until they come to full strength.

'The next stage is to teach them simple commands—to start, to stop, to go left and go right. It's surprising how many different words horsemen use which mean the same thing. The language varies from district to district. I was brought up to the way used in the Whitby district of the North Riding. Gee-up is fairly common throughout for the command to start. Gee-back means turn right and Aargh! means come to the left. It can be quite a job persuading a horse from another district to learn a new language but once they get it right it stays with them for the rest of their days.

'Eventually, a good horse can be driven without using the

53

reins. They are mostly used just to check them a little bit but most real horsemen can train their animals to be almost independent of the reins.

'Once you have brought a heavy horse to that stage, you can be reasonably sure of at least a decade of loyal work and a fair number of foals if it happens to be a mare. Of course, you have an occasional tragedy. A couple of years ago we had a very nice black mare which developed a tumour on the back of her head. Some days she was perfectly well, and others she staggered around because of the pressure on her spinal cord. I talked to the vet and came to the conclusion that one morning we would find her lying dead in a dyke or a pond. I decided that she deserved better than that, so I shot her.

'Now that was a bad day.'

Going lame, however, is the ailment horsemen probably dread most. If its feet or legs fail, a horse is finished. As Geoff points out, a cow can go lame and if it is still capable of yielding five or six gallons of milk a day it's a viable proposition. Similarly, if a lame bullock can still eat and grow fat it is welcome to stay. But a horse must be put down and turned into cans of dog meat.

For a long time, however, there was a much greater peril for horsemen, particularly those who were responsible for keeping the breeds from extinction during the darkest day—finding implements to put behind their horses. Virtually all of the craftsmen and engineers who made the specialized machinery, harness and waggons either went out of business or switched to other work many years ago. In his early days as a farmer, Geoff did his best to build up a store of implements for the future by going round to as many farm sales as he could manage, seeking for cast-off ploughs, cultivators and grass-cutters lying forgotten and gathering cobwebs in the corners of barns. When he was lucky he could pick up machinery invaluable to him for a few shillings. But he increasingly met fierce—indeed, unbeatable—competition from the middle class who raced eagerly round the sales themselves looking for antique ploughs and the like to place decoratively on their front lawns. It still hurts Geoff to think of how much badly-needed machinery rusted away in smart suburbia.

'In fact, I did think at one period that the implement situation might well put a stop to the horse job. It got that serious. But I have changed my mind now—for three reasons.

'First, the steam preservation people have shown us the way by managing to persuade engineers to do one-off jobs. With

55

Geoff in his farmyard with the Ardennes

modern welding techniques you can build castings up, which has also helped smaller firms to be more agreeable when approached for specialized stuff. Second, I've actually had a letter from a small welding fabrication company near Reading asking my advice about the sort of horse-drawn machinery they should think of producing because they were sure that there was going to be a steady demand. I would guess, thankfully, that this sort of thinking will spread.

'Fortunately, there are still a few surviving pockets of genuine, old-style country craftsmen. Some saddlers stayed in touch with their old skills and now they are very busy men, so much so that you have to join a queue if you want a new collar. But, at least, they are still there.

'Blacksmiths, of course, came through it better than anyone because of the fashions for wrought iron and the boom in pony riding. We use one in Market Weighton just down the road who is shoeing ponies all the time. For a while mine were the only heavy horses he was shoeing but he has three or four customers like me now.

'But craftsmen who can still make horse-drawn vehicles are going to be badly needed because waggons are really difficult to find. I know of one wheelwright who made a brand new cart in 1974. It's a beautiful thing, a two-wheel block cart like the one we use except that it's scaled down to two-thirds full size. Sadly, it was made for someone to put on a lawn and stick flowers in. Still, it is comforting to know that there are men

Geoff with his Shires

around capable of building waggons, and I advised that firm in Reading to think first of all in terms of a good, general purpose type of vehicle and a plough.

'I managed to get a new block cart fifteen years ago but my big waggon was made in 1913—not very many of that kind were constructed after the First World War. It will last my time out, though, and maybe my lads' time, too, because they really made waggons in those days.

'I picked up a lot of old machinery at the start of my farming days, including some of the last binders to be made—they stopped in the late forties—and several antiques which are very difficult to date because most of them have been made to a basic pattern for generations. For instance, I have a machine we call a tip-reaper, worked manually, which must be a hundred years old because it is at least two stages back from the binder. We save it now for shows and demonstrations, but it is in good going order and if we ever had a very badly-laid crop of corn that the binder couldn't tackle, then we would put it to work on that.

'I only paid two or three shillings each for most of my collection of implements. Now I see that an old single horse-drawn plough can fetch around twenty-five pounds, which is still very reasonable when you consider what it would cost to make new. And I can take comfort from the knowledge that my implements shed now contains several hundred pounds worth of valuable equipment instead of five pounds worth of scrap iron.

'The third reason for my optimism about the machinery problem is probably the most important of all. There is a move now, partly inspired by the way they do things in America, to go back to putting big teams together—five, six and even eight horses at a time. This means you can use much bigger and heavier implements—tractor implements. We have the power to pull them now if you go about it the right way.'

Geoff is almost certainly responsible for introducing this new, multi-horse work concept to Britain. It started as a typical piece of enterprise, a slender thread seized and steadfastly pursued to fruition. At the Peterborough Show a year or two ago he met an American farmer and eagerly took the chance to discuss methods of working with horses used across the Atlantic. He was already aware that their techniques were, in some ways, much more advanced than those found in this country.

'You see, the conventional English way of ploughing is to use a single furrow walking plough with two, or sometimes three horses abreast. That way you can complete an acre in a day, or up to two if the going is good. But the Americans and Canadians had different ideas right from the start. They could take as much land as they wanted, or could manage, but they didn't have enough labour to work it in the traditional way. So they developed new techniques of hitching and driving and new implements to match. They began to hitch up big teams—four, five and six were commonplace, and they could even go up to twenty horses in the one hitch. In the Mid West and Far West of America, it was usual for one man to work twelve- and sixteen-horse teams.

'Anyway, I knew that they still made gang ploughs in America because the horse situation there never got as low as it did here. I struck up a real friendship with this American farmer, who had a spread in Wisconsin which he runs with Percherons. We wrote to each other and exchanged photographs. Eventually, he was kind enough to buy a gang plough for me and together we arranged transport. He took it apart and packed it into a crate about six feet by four by three, leaving out the pole which was easy to replace over here. He shipped it from Chicago via the Great Lakes and the St Lawrence Seaway to Manchester, and then by road to my farm. It was a fascinating exercise, really. It cost more to bring it from Manchester to Holme-on-Spalding Moor than it did to travel from Chicago to Manchester; sea transport is very cheap.

'But the important thing was the chance to get going with really big teams. We can now plough four acres a day—and a good deal more, if we really set about it—using a five, and occasionally a six-horse team, controlled by just one man. It ploughs two fourteen-inch furrows at a time. That sort of efficiency alters the whole outlook on horses, because a tractor of the type we would use couldn't manage any more without working excessive hours. And, of course, the economics of horses in a situation like that are so much better. If you can manage to work big teams then horses become a very fair proposition even on the major farms, like those that grow grain on a large scale on the chalk lands in the Wolds, and on all the down land in the south of England. It's both practically and technically possible.

'There is no doubt in my mind that the balance is tipping more and more in favour of the horse.'

6

'From Hull, Hell and Halifax Good Lord Deliver Us'

Martinmas is now a defunct feast day, struck from the calendar of this country. Yet in Hull and all along the windswept flatlands it dominates, it is still a significant day, if only in retrospect, because of the decisive effect it once had on the lives of so many local people. It was, indeed, a pivotal date for the whole of the agricultural community for miles around and, typically, they celebrated it on 23rd November—twelve days later than everybody else—and stretched it out to a week. But then Hull and the entire Holderness area has traditionally considered itself apart from the rest of the nation, truculently isolated on its eastern peninsula.

That ancient Yorkshire prayer which heads this chapter was apparently well founded. Halifax was listed because of its infamously busy gibbet which was used by the justices of the town for despatching people found guilty of the slightest crimes; steal anything over the value of fourpence in Halifax and you joined the queue for the drop. Hull's alleged distinction was a uniform meanness and lack of concern for human rights. Anyone who witnessed the way the Hull dock bosses ran their pool of labour, making them virtually beg for work like animals, would say the last remnants of this unsavoury image took a long time to become extinct. It was a degrading spectacle and it was happening until well into the sixties.

On Martinmas Day 1946, Geoff Morton was swabbing decks somewhere out in the Atlantic and Charles Pinney would not be born for another four years. On the Tuesday following the feast a slightly-built seventeen-year-old youth trudged, with hopes high, into the centre of Hull; Ron Creasey, son of a Hull docker, was out to improve himself—and he wanted very badly to work with horses, which was a step up the ladder in agriculture. He considered he could furnish proof of experience—three years hard labour as a general farm hand for which he was initially paid the sum of twenty-two shillings and sixpence a week, less eighteen shillings for board and lodgings.

Ron headed for the wide, stone flag steps of Holy Trinity Church, which was already thronged with other teenage lads. They stood in an untidy line amid a general air of nervous expectancy. There was another group which contrasted sharply against the scene of anxious adolescence. Mostly, they emerged in ones and twos from the neighbouring public houses, mature men with the measured tread of authority. Sternly and slowly, they walked up and down the lines, eyeing and assessing the youths. The occasion was the annual Martinmas Hiring Fair

Ron Creasey at Carr Farm, Flinton, 1947

60

which in Hull incredibly survived until the dawn of the second half of the twentieth century, an uncomfortable echo of the human cattle markets of previous centuries, when the nod of approval from the farmer or his bailiff and a 'fest'—a coin pressed into the hand as a token of contract—meant the difference between survival and starvation for a wretched peasant and his family. Not that the life offered was a bed of bucolic roses, but food at least was assured for another year.

Ron Creasey took his place in the line and waited patiently to be noticed by the bosses and their foremen. His memory of the occasion is crystal sharp today, and curiously he does not express any disapproval about pavement trading in human beings.

'It was my first Martinmas Hiring Fair, you see, and I was keen to get a place. My mate had gone as a third lad to a farm, which meant he would work exclusively with horses. On the

Ron Creasey as a young horseman in the 1950s

bigger places they generally had three men for the horses, working under the foreman. There would be a waggoner, who was head man, third lad and fourth lad. Sometimes there would be a fifth lad, but he would often become the bullocky lad looking after the stock.

'Anyway, I stood there watching the bosses walking up and down, interviewing this or that lad—the first thing they said was, "Now then, do you want hiring, me lad", and then they would tell them what they expected of them and where their farms were situated. Then a man called George Gibson who was foreman of a farm in Flinton came up to me. I knew him because during the war we got bombed in Hull and I was evacuated as a lad to a village called Sproatley, six miles out in the country, and this man's place was in the next village. He looked me over and I told him I wanted fourth lad's job and got it. He also gave me my "fest"—five shillings, which meant I was hired until next Martinmas, 23rd November.'

The deal thus struck meant that Ron was permanently separated from his family because it involved a seven-day week, for a wage of not much more than two pounds a week. And all but seven shillings and sixpence of that was deducted for board and lodgings.

'Aye, and it was an understood thing that you didn't get paid until next Martinmas. But on top of your wage you also got twelve pounds ten shillings a year for working before breakfast and after tea which came out at about five shillings a week. So they let you sub that which was just as well because it was all you had to live on. Your clothes, boot repairs and everything else had to come out of that.'

Flinton was in the middle of a string of East Riding villages where the heavy horse reigned supreme. Ron went to work at Carr Farm, one of a group of major farms owned by the Caleys, a much respected family who are still very prominent in the area. The Caleys shared a common love for horses as well as an appreciation of their working value and Ron estimates that together they ran almost three hundred, mainly Shires or Shires crossed with Clydesdales; and for every four horses they had a lad.

'Three of us slept in a room at the foreman's house—the waggoner, third lad and me. But you couldn't go anywhere from that room except outside. You were never allowed into the living quarters of the foreman and his wife. Some of the lads' rooms just had a ladder and a trap door, but they were generally over the kitchen so it was, at least, warm.

'Discipline was very firm. The day started at half past five when the foreman shouted for us. We would all rush down putting our boots on—we never had time to lace 'em—grabbing our caps and jackets and run past the foreman to the horses as he told the waggoner what harness he wanted on them. There were ten horses in stables and another two in a loose box. When I was fourth lad I would have to muck out four of the stables whilst the other two fed five horses each and then mucked out three stables each. Then I would harness four and they did three apiece. You see, it was considered that the junior lad wasn't capable of feeding 'em properly. Breakfast was at a quarter to seven, and it was marked on some farms by a bell and on others by a whistle. As we ran in, the foreman would meet us with two pints of water. He would then wash as we waited, then the waggoner would wash, then the third lad and then the fourth lad, all in the same two pints of water and strictly in that order, every morning.

'The foreman's wife cooked and served breakfast, all home killed and cured and baked. And you always knew what you were getting. Monday morning meant fat bacon, lean beef, dry bread and a pint of tea, followed by prune pie, fig pie or date pie. All this had to be finished in ten minutes, washing, food eaten and all because you were expected to be back in the stables by five minutes to seven to make sure all the horses' tails were plaited up before they went out.

'By this time the labourers had come in to work and there would be fourteen of us altogether. The foreman would tell them what he wanted them to do, then shout "Get 'em out!" to us. So out clattered the horses and off we went. Maybe we had to bring straw in for the bullocks which meant harnessing three waggons. All the bullocks had to be strawed and fed before eight o'clock when everybody went off to do their main job of the day. We would be sent to plough and the labourers told to hedge or what have you. I was allowed to stay with the horses as long as there were enough horse jobs to do, but if not I'd be put to riddling 'taties or some other general work. We had a hundred acres of 'taties so there was always a lot to riddle.

'I had four horses to look after at all times and they always gave the fourth lad the old 'uns because he wasn't considered experienced enough to handle the youngsters. They weren't pedigree animals but they were big and good. We'd work through the morning ploughing, harrowing or threshing—we did forty days threshing—and always had dinner at the same

Ron Creasey in 1949

time. The horses had to be at the stable door for noon, after being watered at the pond. We would lock them in the stable and go straight into dinner. No water this time for washing your hands, whatever mucky job you'd been doing. The meal was usually beef and fat bacon again but with hot 'taties and gravy, and then some more pie.

'In the summer you would be given plum, apple or bramble pie—whatever fruit was in season—but in winter it would be all dried figs and prunes. Everything was done on a budget because in those days there was no money to spare. And there was always the same priority system at every meal, just like the water for washing. The foreman took his food from the serving dishes first, then the waggoner, third lad and fourth lad; everyone accepted it without question.

'At twenty-five minutes past noon we were all back with the horses again, making sure they had enough to eat, and to save time after tea we got the oats and chaff in. There was a set routine for that, too. Waggoner would get the oats and the lads would carry the chaff. We would do a few other odd jobs and just get nice and finished and having a bit of a sit down when the clock would say one o'clock and there was the foreman shouting "Get 'em out!" again; and out we would stay providing there was enough light until you landed back at the stable door at five o'clock, horses fed and watered; and out would come the foreman with another two pints of water for the same washing procedure.

'The evening meal was meat again and dry bread—always dry bread. But if you had some bread left after eating all the meat, you were allowed to butter it and also have some jam or marmalade. Then we would get the usual pies and perhaps some cake. That was the last food of the day and when you had finished it you were sent back to the horses for grooming and cleaning up.

'By about seven o'clock your time was your own!'

Thirteen-and-a-half hours a day, including the lightning meal breaks, at less than seven shillings (or thirty-five new pence) a day plus the iron discipline may seem an intolerably harsh regime in the light of today's agricultural working conditions; but neither Ron Creasey, nor apparently the hundreds of other youths who experienced it, considered it unreasonable. When he tells his story, not a single complaint drops from Ron's lips. Indeed, he looks back on those days with a kind of affection, and acknowledges that the training he received in the handling of heavy horses was probably unparalleled in Britain. Certainly there was no other reward, for quite apart from the unremitting hard labour the living accommodation provided was Dickensian.

'Well, it certainly wasn't a home from home in the lads' room. The foreman and his wife didn't take us in to be friends—they had never seen us before. The foreman was always called "foreman", even by his wife, and she was always referred to as "missus". We were allowed to call the waggoner by his first name but always took his orders, just as the fourth lad would take orders from the third lad. You accepted this because you knew your turn would come one day to give the orders.

'There wasn't much comfort in the room, either. In fact, there was nothing except beds and one chair. There was no tap in the room, no toilet and no electricity at first. We were given one hurricane lamp so that we could see up the stairway. All the beds were double beds because you were expected to sleep with somebody. Nobody thought anything about it, but I remember students who occasionally came to stay for a brief spell at the farm being shocked when they realized they were expected to share a bed with another lad. They were also a bit taken aback when they saw nobody had pyjamas. Everybody slept in their working shirts. You see, we only ever had one set of clothes to wear because the other would be in the wash. The foreman's wife never washed for you, of course, but it was always possible to find a labourer's wife to do it for you. Generally, two lads would come to an arrangement with one woman—

65

but she would have to agree to wait until Martinmas before she got paid. The price was generally two pounds ten shillings for the year. We even had our Sunday paper delivered on the same sort of deal, paying the newsagent at Martinmas.

'There wasn't much for us lads to do to amuse ourselves when we did get some time off. Flinton had nothing to offer and if you took the road out one way you would come to another village exactly the same. It was even the same distance—two-and-a-half miles. The one thing we all possessed though was a bicycle. So all the lads around would meet up and pass the time as best we could. We were all in the same financial circumstances so you had to think real hard before parting with any brass. That meant the pubs were out so we stood around a lot at street corners or went to one of the stables and played darts or cards. Sometimes when you got a bit older there would be a bit of skylarking around with the local girls.

'Mind, you were expected to stay single in the East Riding if you worked among horses. There were married waggoners, but not many, and they were sometimes expected to take a house and board the lads if they did wed. Pay for a waggoner was about four pounds a week. One of the Caleys had a married waggoner for years because his son did the foreman's job. It never happened in my time, but I recall some of the older men tell about the times when hiring really was hiring and if you got married as a lad you had to live apart. This happened most frequently when a lad got a lass into trouble and had to marry her; but they couldn't live together as man and wife until the following Martinmas. More often than not the girl would be hired as a maid somewhere.

'Weekend was the time when we had a proper chance to do a bit of courting. On Saturdays you were allowed off at dinner time and you had a couple of hours to yourself until four o'clock when you did your horses again. Sunday mornings we had a lie-in. We didn't have to get up until quarter to seven. We would feed the horses and do a few odd jobs for half an hour, but no work in the fields. Then the waggoner would look at his watch and shout to the foreman's missus to start getting our breakfast. Fifteen minutes later we went in to find it all ready. Usually we had eggs and bacon on a Sunday morning, but we didn't look forward to it because it was still the same old bacon. I remember once on a Sunday morning the missus being very apologetic because she hadn't got any bacon boiled and asked if we would mind beans on toast. She thought it wrong that there was no meat for us but we were all highly delighted because it made such a change. But I had no complaints about the food we were given. It suited me and we ate it all because all the hard work we did in the fresh air made you very hungry.

'We were very fit, too. Quite apart from the work with the horses which was strenuous enough, we had to carry big weights around. Oats came in bags weighing a hundredweight-and-a-half, barley in sixteen stones, peas in nineteens and beans in twenties. You were expected to hump all these bags to the grainery and a normal carry was around fifty yards, then up thirteen steps and another ten yards. Two of you would do that all day long, passing each other on the way. But everyone was tough and strong, particularly the foreman. He was a man no bigger than me—hardly five foot six inches—but he could get under farm waggons weighing twenty-five hundredweight, lift them off the ground and walk sideways.

'I remember another man in the early days, an old labourer called Ted Simpson who swore he could lift himself in a scuttle when he was a young man. A scuttle is a round container with two handles which we used to fill with corn to carry to the bullocks. A nice old fellow was Ted, but he would insist it was possible so we youngsters used to persuade him to show us. And he would get in a scuttle and really lift hard and we would urge him on, shouting out that it was half an inch off the ground as he got redder and redder in the face. He used to tell us some tall stories did that man.

'There used to be some remarkable characters around in those days. Come haytime and harvest the casual Irish labourers would arrive and instead of being fourteen men setting out to work in the morning there would be as many as forty. It made a change for us, too, because the Irishmen would be boarded in the lads' room and we were moved into the foreman's house proper. And they would have to wait until we had taken our food before they got theirs. That was a busy time for the foreman's wife. As well as providing the usual meals she would have to bring us each a sandwich and a pint of tea to the fields in the morning, and half a fruit pie and a pint of tea again in the afternoon. We would all sit down in the stubble and eat this and try our best to get the foreman spinning a yarn about the old days. If we could get him going it would mean an extra five minutes sit down.

'But some foremen were as keen as mustard and you could get away with nothing. I remember one old timer who worked for the Caleys for about forty years. One harvest-time they ran short of labour and Charlie went down to ask the local publican

67

Haytime in the 1950s, East Yorkshire

if he would come and help for half a day, for which he would be paid. Well, he came and they got to the stage where one load had been finished and there was nothing to do for a few minutes. So the publican sat down for a rest on a waggon pole. When the foreman saw him he called out, "I shouldn't sit down there, Jim!" And when the publican pointed out that there was nothing to do at that moment the foreman said, "Yes, but you want to be stood up when there is!" I went out with the same old man one day to hoe mangles together with the waggoner, a labourer and another hired lad. Now it was the custom that when you did a turn—that's once up and once down—you could stop, cut your tobacco twist and fill your pipe. But me and the other lad didn't smoke so we just stood and waited for the others who did. And he turned on us and said, "Don't you lads be stood there doing nowt!" If we had been cutting twist or rolling a cigarette it would have been all right, but he just couldn't abide people hanging around being inactive whatever the situation.

'He once told us that in his early days if a lad did something wrong the foreman would go to him and shout, "Get in the house to bed!" and up to bed they had to go in disgrace, lads of sixteen and seventeen.'

68

The one relief in the relentless cycle of work and discipline for a hired lad came, of course, at Martinmas. They were handed their year's wage, less subs, and given a whole week off—on full pay. It was traditional to make the most of it. Throughout the East Riding their short parole was known as 'Martinmas Madness' as most youths went home and made merry with their money, organizing parties, drinking beer, chasing girls and generally having a blissful time. Some of them never went to bed throughout the whole week.

On one of his first Martinmas breaks, Ron Creasey made an unusual foray into the outside world. He treated himself to a week at Butlins and for the first time in his life tasted cornflakes. 'Aye, now that was a real novelty for a hired lad.'

7

The Lone Campaigner

For those horse enthusiasts who today plaintively ask why, if there were so many hundreds of farmhands working with heavy horses every day of their lives, was there not a thunderous shout of protest from them when the extermination of the heavy horse began. Ron Creasey has a simple answer.

'A lot of 'em were as sick as hell of horses, particularly the older men. It was no fun at times, you know. At the spring of the year your feet ached and were full of blisters because you had been walking from the last week in February, all through March and April and half-way into May; more often than not in the pouring rain, so at times you wished your horses in hell.

'To plough an acre you walk eleven miles and they wanted an acre a day from you. Gib-harrowing was a bit better because it was dead slow walking but when we went out with a Cambridge roller they would tell us to get some music into it. They wanted twenty acres a day with the Cambridge so you and the horses had to go flat out; and this went on for days and days.

'Horses had their funny days just like people, you know, when they would be plain awkward. I'll always remember the time I took out a particular mare called Daisy to put down top-dressing with a drill on the corn. We were always given a set target and I was told to do twenty acres a day, putting down about two hundredweight of dressing per acre. So we really had to go at it. Now this mare was known to be a kicker and apparently the foreman told one of the labourers that she would get us before I had finished the job. Mind, she could really shift; but what a time I had with the beast. Every time Daisy turned,

70

her tail started twirling round and she would pee all over me!

'Then one morning it happened, pretty much as the foreman said it would. She kicked as hard as she could and jumped straight out of the shafts. I was stood at the back of the drill and there was the horse—facing me. She had crossed these tubular shafts and her head was sticking through the bend. So I got her out and trailed her back to the yard. It was half past eight in the morning and they all saw me coming. Foreman shouted "Put the thing away!" and asked what had happened. When I told him he was quite reasonable about it—didn't even swear, but then he was a Sunday School teacher and never did. He told me to go back, take the shafts off and carry them on my back down to the blacksmith two miles down the road. I took my bike. The blacksmith straightened them out and I dragged the shafts all the way back where the foreman had a fresh horse waiting for me. I had to go straight out again top-dressing.

'On the other hand, I worked regularly with another horse,

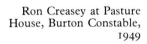

Ron Creasey at Pasture House, Burton Constable, 1949

71

a big gelding called Cobby. He must have been all of eighteen hands and he was a masterpiece, a real clever animal. A marvellous drill horse, he could walk straight, he could walk fast and to cap it all he was a check horse, which meant you could drive him with just one rein.

'Funny thing about the check rein. It was used everywhere from Middle Holderness down to Spurn Point. But from Middle Holderness back to Beverley it was unknown. Useful thing it was because it left one hand free so you just pulled to go "hove", which is left, and checked to go "gee back", which is right. You would harness up another two horses with Cobby, put a false line on them and he would drive them along with him. But you only had direct contact with one mouth— Cobby's.

'Eventually I could work that horse without any reins at all, doing endless jobs. I just told him what I wanted him to do. If we were drilling I used to climb into a waggon by the side of the field and be opening some bags as I directed him to walk towards me with a drill, turn round and back up to the waggon. Then I filled the drill up again, gave him the command to start and off he would go without me touching him. What a horse he was! He could understand from the tone of my voice exactly what he had to do.

'But even Cobby wasn't good for everything. You could not drill mangles or swedes with him because to do that you had to put a stick to a horse's mouth and hang on to it with your hand. Trouble was his head wouldn't respond to his body and up it would go in the air. Horses are like people—some people just don't have the temperament for some jobs. And one horse would take to one man and not to another, and vice versa. But a real good horse was one which would go fast and straight. You could put any horse into a scruffler which works in between the rows, but to do a shimming job you had to pick your animal. A good shim horse was one which would keep in one row during a two-row shim and not shove his arse over and walk with two legs in one run and two legs in the other.'

During his years in service to the Caley family, Ron Creasey made swift progress. He became third lad after a year and then moved smoothly into the waggoner's position at another Caley farm. He was a natural horse man—basically still is—but even before the time he had reached a position of authority the roof had started to fall in on his world. By 1947 the tractor began to cast its deadly shadow on the stable door. Ron resisted with a rare ferocity.

Ron Creasey hoeing
mangolds in the 1950s

'There is a place for a tractor on a farm. We had one from
1937 and everyone was pleased with it, both men and horses.
It was a real partnership because the tractor could take some
of the particularly hard work out of certain jobs. For instance
binders—for cutting the corn—made killing work for horses.
We were all right because we rode on their backs. And then
there was the ploughing of fallow land. In that strong Holderness clay it was a terrible job to drag out big boulders, but
tractors could take over both jobs and everyone was pleased.

'Suddenly the horse became the dog's-body, set to do all the
mucky jobs. And the tractor men were saying it was time to
get all those land crabs off the place. There was a hell of a row,
I can tell you. It got very bad tempered at times, almost to the
point of fighting. The same argument was going on in farms
all round the country, I suppose, with men like me—not
mechanically minded—fighting to the last.'

Ron, a practical man at all times, decided one summer on
a lone campaign to demonstrate to everyone that horses could
perform just as well as tractors. After working his full day, he
would take a team out after he had finished his evening meal
at 6 pm, and work through until ten at night; and he kept it
up for weeks.

'In fact, I was really trying to prove that we could beat some of them tractors and, for once, I was glad when it rained because that's when we were masters of the situation; the tractor had to stop and we kept going.'

His bosses were impressed, but it was a Canute-like gesture. Gradually, the horses Ron cared for day and night went down to the sales, already teeming with the loyal cast-offs from a score of surrounding farms. To some extent, the Caley family shared Ron's views and most of the other much smaller farms became fully mechanized long before they slowly capitulated to the internal combustion engine.

'They began to sell them in lots of about twenty. I remember on Good Friday 1947, we packed off twenty-two, and every horse had been bred on the farm. The following year twenty-five went. Most of them were bought for their meat at about forty pounds a time, but some of the better horses were reprieved because the railway people stepped in and bought them to work at York. But the top price was only around seventy-five guineas.

'The Caleys couldn't bear to part with them all, and right up to 1961 still had a few—and they kept on proving their worth, particularly during the bad weather in winter. By that time everything had been reorganized and I ended up in charge of all the stock—three or four hundred bullocks, six hundred ewes and a hundred sows. I was also responsible for all the potatoes, had a gang of my own and ran all the casual labour at picking time.

'I was married by then and living in a tied house; but by 1961 I'd had enough of working in Holderness. We were still at it all hours and I thought there ought to be something more to life than that. There wasn't much point in looking for a place on another farm in the area because they were all very much the same, so I took a job as a shepherd in the Cotswolds.

'In one way I suppose it was a step down, but not financially because nobody in agriculture got paid much in the East Riding. I could do the shepherding job all right because I'd been organizing sheep shearing three times a year for a long time and could run a dog. But it was a shock when I started down there. I would never have believed that a place could be run so slap-happy. In the morning when they told you what job they wanted done, they would even explain how to get to it, which field to go through; and if they told you to go and fence, they would remind you to take a hammer with you!'

This came hard to a man who had been giving orders to forty men every day for the last ten years. And being a Yorkshireman in the total sense of the word he spoke his mind to these strange southerners with their sloppy, gentle ways.

'I'd been there about a week when I told the boss what I thought. I said that I'd never been so surprised in my life at the way he ran his farm and that he wouldn't be able to run a hundred acres back in Yorkshire.'

Not surprisingly, Ron moved on. But not back to Yorkshire. His wife had taken to the voluptuous appeal of the south, particularly the climate, and he put even more distance between himself and his homeland.

'I applied for a job as a bailiff which was advertised in the paper. It was at a 500-acre farm owned by a newspaper man in Catsfield just outside Battle in Sussex. Now I got it, without

The young Shires Ron Creasey took over in Sussex

really knowing what you were supposed to do as bailiff. It's a southern word meaning manager. When I got there I found I was expected to buy and sell cattle, buy and sell corn and just about run the place completely. Well, this was something I had never done in my life before. Back in Yorkshire the bosses had never let us in on the secrets of these things. There had been no question of their employees, even senior men like me, being involved in the trading of animals or fodder or anything about management, because it was none of our business.

'So I bought the *Farmers' Weekly* and learned fast. I'm still there, running a herd of Sussex cattle and a flock of pedigree sheep. It's a nice place.'

When he exiled himself to the Cotswolds, Ron Creasey—for the first time in fifteen years—wasn't among horses. It must have left a painful gap in his life although with typical Yorkshire pride, he declared that he 'could take 'em or leave 'em'. But when he found that on the farm adjoining at Catsfield there was a trainer with eighteen racehorses he went calling and they let him exercise the hack. And then he was told about another farm two or three miles down the road which actually had a couple of Shire horses. It must have been a joyful moment for him, particularly when he heard they were having real trouble with them.

'Seems that every time they tried to do any work with these Shires they would run away and get into such a state that they couldn't do anything with them. They were young horses, good black 'uns, and gentle enough until somebody tried to yoke them.

'So I thought, well I'll just go down and have a look at this place.'

It must have been an enormous relief to the owners of the Shires when Ron Creasey marched up and took over. And how he must have relished exercising all his old skills again.

'I got 'em going all right; they wanted to start showing them so I persuaded the owner to go with me back to Yorkshire and buy a Yorkshire waggon. We brought it back and renovated it at nights. Then we took it out with the Shires—first to the show at Regent's Park, then to the South of England and Kent shows.

'I borrowed another horse and showed them how we did it in the East Riding, riding and driving three. We came in for a lot of criticism from these south country fellows just because it was different. But at all three shows the judges came up to me individually and said they had never ever seen three horses

77

Ron Creasey today, riding one of his three-horse team

driven like that with a man riding and how pleased they were to see something completely different. And they had been judging horses for about forty years.'

A remarkable man, Ron Creasey; and along the rolling Sussex downs, he must be a curious transplant in the eyes of the locals, with his uncompromising directness and unique Yorkshire ways. But Ron is one of the last of a special breed, every one of his five foot six inches permanently honed by one of the toughest and most complete systems of farming in Europe, from which he graduated with honours and which no longer exists. The south is fortunate to have him.

8

The Master of Edingale

Very occasionally—maybe just once or twice a decade—those heavily involved, like the writer, in the rural affairs of this country experience a culture shock of the most fascinating and memorable kind. Suddenly one is rivetingly aware of having stumbled into a situation of genuine rarity and one can almost identify with the archaeologist who unexpectedly unearths an artefact which advances his knowledge of peoples and customs long extinct.

Edingale House Farm dominates the tiny and isolated village of Edingale, buried in the agricultural heart of the midlands in Staffordshire, too insignificant to be noticed by some maps and linked tenuously to the outside world by slender, sinuous and closely-hedged lanes. To be a guest at this farm is like stepping into a sepia photograph taken half a century or more ago and watching it come to life around you.

The outlying barns, byres, stables and yards make no discernible concession whatsoever to the twentieth century, and they are attended by three dourly preoccupied men, none of whom have worked anywhere else since they left school and who have a combined total of service at Edingale House Farm which exceeds 130 years. But they are beardless youths when compared to the man who greets you in the cobbled yard, elderly collie by his side, and leads you into the enormous rambling farmhouse which has stood for around three centuries. The kitchen is aglow from the enamelled, solid fuel cooking range over which is bent an aproned, white-haired lady, wife of one of those faithful farm servants, and the air is pungent with the odours of roasting joints, fresh vegetables on the boil and steaming puddings. In the sitting-room adjoining the solidly-furnished smaller dining-room (the walls are decked with framed photographs, not one of which was taken less than three decades ago) the sherry is served by the glow of an open fire.

Privileged visitors will be shown over the house—room after spacious room, crowded with elegant reminders of a forgotten age. There are wig stands, hand-carved cabinets with special drawers for herbs, exquisite display cases glittering with sterling silver; all antiques—but not when they were bought.

At the table, there is a ritual which matches the atmosphere exactly. The head of the household solemnly carves the joint and hands each plate to his wife to add the vegetables and serve to the guests. The portions for the men are significantly larger than those for the women. When the plates are nearly empty, second helpings of vegetables are offered to the guests and then, finally, to the host. His wife leans forward and says:

'Would you like some more, master?'

To those sitting around the table for the first time, it is quite a moment. And for a split second, forks full of roast lamb freeze between plate and mouth and eyes meet questioningly. Master? Did one hear a'right? A few minutes later comes confirmation.

'Will you be having pudding, master?'

To be sure, Edward Jocelyn Holland is the master of Edingale House Farm, and has been for the last sixty years and more. Everyone on the farm calls him 'master'—but not from fear. Jos Holland is far from being a martinet. On the contrary, he is small, softly spoken, courteous and totally benevolent. He is called master because that's the way of things on his farm. It's to do with respect and tradition and it doesn't matter what other people get up to across the rolling fields and over the horizon. Women's Lib, men on the moon, faster-than-sound travel and power to the workers may be commonplace in those strange, far-off places but at Edingale House relationships, attitudes and manners were cast in iron before Mrs Pankhurst even thought of fastening her chains around the railings of Westminster, and clearly nothing is going to change them now.

Jos Holland is a truly remarkable man. In 1979 he will enter his ninetieth year, and he can remember joining in the national rejoicing when Mafeking was relieved during the Boer War before the turn of the century. Yet he still rises at 5.15 am each day and often works for sixteen out of the twenty-four hours.

And his influence extends far beyond the boundaries of his farm. He is the acknowledged elder statesman of as uncompromising a group of men as you are every likely to meet in this land, and his flag of office can be seen gyrating above the roof of his biggest barn—a weather vane crowned by the wrought-iron figure of a Shire horse. He is the oldest, and the most venerated member of the Council of the Shire Horse Society, which was founded in 1878, a mere eleven years before he was born. He possibly knows more about Shire horses than anyone else in the world. For more than half a century he has been an outstandingly successful breeder of Shires, and he and his loyal group of retainers still work with fourteen prime examples of the breed, including four magnificent stallions. It is worth travelling a long way to experience the control Jos has over his horses. He strolls to a five-barred gate, a diminutive figure, calls out in a casual manner, and an eighteen-hand black stallion weighing around a ton will immediately stop grazing, lumber up to him and frisk around like a gigantic puppy dog.

Yet the start Jos had in life was scarcely calculated to be a springboard to success. His father—a farmer, naturally—died before he was three, he had two elder brothers (and in those days, the elder sons expected to get the lion's share of any inheritance), and he can claim without fear of contradiction that he received less formal education than anybody else he knows. Born on a farm near Crewe, he didn't even start school until his family moved to Newport in Shropshire when he was eight-and-a-half.

'I went until I was eleven and then I got ringworms on my head and I couldn't go for a year. Before I was able to go back we moved to another farm near Stafford and I never went to school again. We were very busy on the new place so it kept being put off and I certainly didn't want to start again after such a gap. It wasn't compulsory in those days, you know. It was still the nineteenth century.'

Jos, his mother and one brother came to Edingale House Farm in 1909. The eldest son had married and left before the new move and two years later after all those setbacks, Jos's first real chance in life arrived. His other brother also left to get married and he became the man of the house, with all that implied in this society, at the early age of twenty-one. Eight years later he took a wife, a local girl and, as custom dictated in those days, his mother and his two sisters went to live elsewhere to leave the field clear for the new mistress of Edingale—and her master.

Jos Holland and his bride,
taken on honeymoon in
Bournemouth

Mrs Alice Holland is one year older than her husband and
equally active and hardworking. You cannot be idle and a successful farmer—or a farmer's wife. To this day, she fondly
remembers their honeymoon, a blissful few days in Bournemouth.

'He told me to make a fuss about it because we might not
get the chance to go away on holiday again; and he was right—
we have been married fifty-nine years now and we haven't been
away since then.'

Jos was too busy building up a prosperous farm even to think
about such luxuries. He had two hundred acres of strong, clay
land to work. He planted corn and a few root crops then decided
it was better suited to growing cattle—big-boned cattle—and
seeded it for turf. Naturally, he worked his farm with horses.
And it soon became obvious that he was gifted with the ability
to pick out a really good horse from a bunch of gangling year-
lings—something for which he is justly celebrated now. Also,
he was an extremely astute businessman.

'Together with my brothers, I always used to break in colts
for working when I was a lad. Ordinary farm horses, not Shires.
We would keep them for about five or six years and then sell
them for town work. I didn't know much about Shires until
1920 when I went to the London Show with a member of the
Froggatt family, who were very well known in the Shire world.
That's when the interest started for me. I began to make it

82

my business to get to know the breed and two years later I bought a Shire mare called Pipe Ridware Bloom which had done a lot of winning about Edingale. I paid £215 for her at a farm sale. That was a lot of money fifty-five years ago, but then her filly foal the year before had won the Lichfield Show and made £150. She was in foal when I got her and gave birth to a filly, but it died of pneumonia after a few days. So I went and bought the foal which had won Lichfield, and was now a yearling, for £205. I kept them for two years but lost them both within a fortnight. The mare got kicked by another horse and fetched up with a broken leg, her foal stepped on a nail and the wound went septic.

Jos Holland judging

'It was a bad start.'

An understatement which is typical of the man. It was a disaster of enormous proportions because Jos admits that he was not well off at the time, certainly not rich enough to lose money in such large amounts. It was sufficient to put an ordinary farmer off Shire horses for life, but, fortunately for the general welfare of the breed, Jos was determined to recoup his losses and went to the next Peterborough Show. This time he bought a stallion, a very significant step. It proved to be the foundation of his stud which was built principally on his uncanny knack for spotting colts which would grow into outstanding stallions. He just didn't have the money to wait until the colt became a man and his looks and ability clear for all to see.

His first stallion was a two-year-old called Cippingham Draughtsman for which he paid £150. The following spring he sold him for £350 back to the original owner!

'That really started me off. I began to buy six colts a year, mostly at Peterborough, rear them until they were about three years old, and then sell them. I was very lucky—I picked out one or two of the best sires and bought their foals. During the next fifteen years or so I sold not many short of fifty young stallions at an average of well over £200 each.'

A gross turnover of more than ten thousand pounds—and Jos was simultaneously rearing a pedigree dairy herd, prize sheep and Tamworth pigs. He also had a brood mare which was producing good foals. In 1931, one of the stallions Jos had bred and sold took a second in London and one of his own mares gained a fifth (rising to a second in 1932, after he had sold her). Then his mare, Thurviston Rosebud, secured the coveted first. Each of these three Shires brought him £275.

Spectacular success of this kind in such a short time had the top breeders beating a path to Edingale. Among them were the Forshaws, proprietors of the biggest stud in the country, with around seventy stallions, no less, and Mr Balderston, who probably had the second biggest. Altogether Mr Balderston bought seventeen stallions from Jos, who always seemed to own just the kind of horse the big men were looking for. They were so impressed by the constant level of quality that on one occasion Mr Tom Forshaw bought one from Jos without even seeing it first.

'One night he rang me up to ask if I knew where he could quickly find a small stallion, sixteen hands to sixteen one, clean-legged with no white on them and a good mover. He had a customer in Ireland. Oddly enough, I'd bought a stallion just like that only two or three days before, so I told him that I had one which might suit. So he said, "Right—can you get him to my place before nine o'clock tomorrow morning." He lived in a place called Carlton, near Newark in Nottinghamshire. I had a waggon on the road at 5.30 am. Just before he was put in the waggon the horse shed a shoe, but the driver had been a blacksmith previously so he put the shoe back on and still had the stallion at Carlton fifteen minutes early. He was on the way to Ireland the same day, and Mr Forshaw was so delighted with the horse that he rang me again in the evening and said he was going to pay me more than the price I was asking! The people who bought him later said he was the best Shire in Ireland.

'He was a very good man was Mr Tom Forshaw, one of the best I ever knew. He bought a fair number of stallions off me over the years and he never argued about the price—just asked me for "luck" money back. I remember I gave him twenty pounds "luck" once on a deal for £275. Very religious person too, and always did the right thing; I think he sang in the same choir for sixty-seven years.

'Of course, they were a different breed of men in those days, farmers and farm workers. We all had to work a lot harder and a lot longer hours. Men had a deal more strength, too, because the least of them were expected to plough an acre a day. They didn't get much money, either. When we took this farm over we paid the hands fifteen shillings a week. A bit later I hired a man from a neighbouring farm and paid him sixteen shillings, but what a worker he was. Once with a pair of horses he ploughed me a ten-and-a-half acre field, starting on the Monday and finishing at two o'clock the following Saturday—and all for sixteen shillings.'

Physical prowess, it seems, was very important to men in agriculture half a century ago. Not only did it make you a more valuable asset in the fields, it was also a matter of masculine pride. All men—workers and masters—were judged by their muscle and even Jos Holland, small though he was, trained himself to be able to lift and carry a bag of wheat weighing 252 pounds. But that was nothing compared to the prodigious feats performed by others of his generation.

'Trials of strength were commonplace in the old days. I've known three men in my time who could carry five hundred-weights on their back. One was a miller called Willie Howells at Great Hayward Mill on the canal near Stafford, who one day round about 1930 had a bet with the driver of the cart who took the corn around to the farms—another big man. The winner

Ancient and Modern—Jos Holland and one of his magnificent Shires contrasts with a brand new tractor

was to be the one who carried the most bags of wheat from the narrow boat on the canal to the mill. Well, they started carrying these bags one at a time, and for a while it was neck and neck. Then Willie grabbed a piece of harness and strapped two bags together—total weight 504 pounds—hoisted them on to his back and strode off to the mill. The other fellow swore in amazement and gave in there and then.

'I met Willie Howells first when I was just a lad. We used to take our sows to a boar he kept at his mill and on one occasion me and another lad were trying unsuccessfully together to get a sow back on to the cart to take home. Willie came over to ask what the trouble was and we told him we couldn't manage to lift this big sow, which was at least twelve score—240 pounds and more. He asked us to lift up the net on the cart, leaned over the pig, picked it up and threw it on. He was a mighty man.

'But some of those big men also had big thirsts, and it caused their downfall eventually because the beer was stronger in those days, too. To be able to down a lot of drink was another thing to put you in the limelight then. I knew one man, six foot two and eighteen stone, who came from a very well-to-do family and reckoned he could drink forty pints of beer a day. His family eventually turned him out and disowned him and the last I heard he was living in a caravan, sporting a gold medal which he won in a competition in London for drinking the most beer in the least time. He put down thirty pints in thirty minutes and carried off the medal and prize money amounting to £150. He was a very good horse man in his time—travelled a stallion for me once—and used to make a bit of money plaiting tails and manes at the shows. I think his family made him an allowance but they never took him back and he never married. I did see him again at a show in 1977. He must be eighty now and he's looking a lot better than he did because he has cut down to four pints a day.'

In his quiet way, Jos Holland has performed a much more laudable feat than any of these giants of the past. He has outlived most of them, and looks twenty years younger than his eighty-seven years—which is even more remarkable in the light of the fact that doctors almost gave him up for lost before the turn of the century.

'I was a very delicate child. I had pneumonia twice and suffered badly from asthma and bronchitis. The doctors told my mother that if she could keep me going until I was nine I might survive to manhood. And the older I got, the healthier I became until I cast off all my complaints.'

Today, he looks good to reach 109, and he is still conducting a thriving business breeding and selling Shire horses, mostly black and all of outstanding quality. One of his mares recently brought a bid of more than two thousands pounds and a filly foal not much less. His three senior stallions are renowned for siring champions and he also keeps seven mares to maintain a yearly crop of foals.

But his pride and joy is a superb beast called Edingale Mascot which he obviously believes is the best young Shire stallion in Britain. It took the second prize and reserve champion award at a recent Peterborough Show and clearly has far to go. Jos values Mascot at five thousand pounds, and is looking forward eagerly to supervising his progress—as he nears the completion of his sixth decade as a breeder of Shire horses.

9

God Meant Shire Horses to Walk!

It is is a mistake to assume that all the expert handlers of heavy horses are necessarily countrymen, born next to a stable and raised in the harness room. On the contrary, it is hard to deny that some men who scarcely ever see more than a scrap of greenery, who have lived all their lives against red brick horizons, their ears filled with the roar of the internal combustion engine instead of birdsong and their eyes for ever meeting factory chimneys instead of trees, are among the finest horsemen in the land.

Albert Hobson is one man with very definite views about this point; colourfully definite, in fact, but then he is an archetypal Yorkshireman, one of a breed celebrated for being positive about all things.

'The best horsemen came out of towns. That may sound odd but there can be no argument about it. I have lots of farmer friends who talk about how good they were with horses—but it's easy to be good in a ten-acre field. I would like to have seen 'em put horses through a town like we had to do in the old days with trams ringing their bells on one side of you, and cars trying to get past on the other. That was the real test of a man's ability to control a horse.'

Albert himself was born in the Headrow, Leeds, which is as close as Yorkshire ever gets to Piccadilly. The year was 1926, when the horse still had the edge over the engine, and he has never moved from the centre of the city. Today, he is the Supervisor of Horse Transport for Tetley's Brewery in Leeds, a title which amuses him.

'It means I'm t'head horseman, lad,' he says.

He is a very down-to-earth character working for a brewery which doesn't believe in keeping one set of heavy horses for work and another set for showing. They have eight young Shires, four grey and four bay, and they all earn their living hauling beer. It means they don't get as much publicity as some of the other breweries because their showing activities are mainly confined to Yorkshire. The Royal and the annual affair at Peterborough are shows they don't bother about.

But unlike a lot of their rivals who got rid of all their horses during the decimating switch to motor transport and have only reinstated them in recent years, Yorkshire's biggest brewery, founded in 1823, always kept faith with the Shire. Never in a century-and-a-half have they been without them. You do not get people in Leeds gaping at the proud sight of a pair of Shires clattering around the streets like you do in other cities because it has never been anything other than a regular thing.

Albert is the son of a remarkable man, once known throughout the Leeds area as Knacker Dick. He was a coal merchant and general dealer whose working life was geared to horses.

'He dealt in anything—you had to in those days to make a living—but he was called Knacker because of his ability to buy horses that looked fit only for the knacker's yard and making them good again. In a way he was a forerunner of these people who rescue old cars from scrap yards and restore them. He was a dab hand at it. His secret was to feed them little but often and it was wonderful the way they came on.

'I have no idea why they called him Dick because his real name was George. They even called me Young Dick as a lad and some of the old-timers still refer to me as Dick.

'My very earliest memory concerned horses. I couldn't have been more than three or four but I can clearly remember being in my father's stable in Mark Lane just off the Headrow, and listening to him bargain for and buy a horse called Ginger. The man he bought it off was the first knacker man in this town, John Moody, better known as One-Eyed John and a very keen man. They used to say he could see better with one eye than most men can with two. He bought a lot of his horses from the two rival evening newspapers in Manchester, the *News* and the *Chronicle*. They needed to be able to pull a cart, full of newspapers, and be capable of a mile in three minutes. If they missed a train they had to be fast enough to beat it to the next station. I believe they did regular time trials with those horses and if they failed to do the three-minute mile they would be sold to One-Eyed John.

Two of the Tetley horses out delivering beer

'It was all horses in those days, of course, and my family was involved with them from way back. My grandfather used to drive a horse for Leeds Corporation. You really had to know how to handle horses in the cities because there were so many hazards. Many's the time I've seen an iron-tyred Co-op milk float go over whilst trying to get back home too fast after finishing delivering. One wheel would slide on the granite sets and hit the tram lines going down the middle of the road and the cart would be on its side in the gutter with the horse still going strong, dragging the shafts behind it. Horsemen and tramdrivers didn't get on too well and there were one or two accidents. I remember once when I was very young my father limping into the house on a stick, with his leg and arm all bandaged up. A tram had run away out of control when he was leading his cart down Headingley Lane—it was Ginger in the shafts—

92

and smashed him up against the wall. The cart finished up in bits and my father sent flying, but the horse got away with it. The police kept it in their stables until the next day.

'But he was a hard man, my Dad. You had to be to work horses like he did. When I was still at school a lot of ponies were imported from Russia and Iceland, usually pacers of about twelve hands with a rounded gait like trotting ponies. They were very popular with ice-cream men, I recall. Well, we got one and I was told to take him up the road and try him out. I had a terrible time with the thing and came back home with tears in my eyes—I was only twelve at the time. "What's up?" said my Dad. I told him the horse was bad in traffic and frightened to death of trams.

'"Get back up on that cart," roared my Dad, and he grabbed hold of the reins. I'm not kidding you, by the time he had finished with that horse it would have been glad to get on one of those trams. By heck, did he straighten him out. He taught me a lesson which I keep on trying to pass on to my lads. If you have to use a whip, use it only once. But use it properly. Same with children.

'There wasn't a horse on God's earth that my father was afraid of. He could handle the lot. But he didn't like donkeys much because one bit off half his thumb.'

Knacker Dick Hobson was very much a man of his time, one of a generation of larger-than-life characters who flourished in the horse world between the wars—powerful men, with a keenly-developed sense of pride. There was a constant atmosphere of competition—they appeared to feel the regular need to prove themselves and their animals. This led to some spirited encounters, one of which became an outstanding memory of Albert Hobson's childhood.

'This happened down at the old muck dock down in Shannon Street. That's where the railway cattle trucks used to come in and get loaded up with pig and horse manure. Everyone kept pigs and horses then and there were men called muck-pluggers who would come with their carts, and give you a shilling to clear out your midden. Then they took it down to the muck dock and sent it off to farmers and market gardeners by rail. You could smell that place a mile away. Now, there was a carting firm called Thomas Dean's in Pontefract Lane and they had a lot of big shivering horses. A "shiv" was an animal which had something wrong with its spine which meant it couldn't back up properly—but they would go forward for ever when told.

A Tetley four-in-hand at the Pickering traction engine rally, 1972

'They had one pair of old geldings called Dick and Jerry which pulled in tandem, real good shivers. Jerry had a hole in his face where he had been struck by lightning and they covered it with a leather shield. Dick was the chain horse—the one in the lead—and a little man called Albert Varley used to work 'em down at the muck dock. One day there a man came on the dock with a beautiful bay mare. By heck, she was a stamp of a thing, five years old and full of power and go. Her owner,

a young man, was very proud of her and turned his nose up at Dick and Jerry. He told Albert to get those old crabs out of the way and claimed his mare could shift more than Dick and Jerry pulling together. That started a fierce argument which ended with Albert telling the young man to put his money where his mouth was. So there and then they arranged a tug-of-war between the mare and Dick, winner to take both horses.

95

'The two horses were chained together, arse to arse. Both men agreed there were to be no sticks or whips—just word of mouth. So it started. They bid them go, and the two horses both laid into their collars. After a bit the bay mare began trembling with the strain, and old Dick started to groan. Now when a horse starts to groan, it's putting some power out. Then this mare made one fatal mistake. She lifted her leg to go. Albert spotted this and as her leg was in the air he just growled, "Dick, my lad!" Dick went "urrgh", and he had her. Dragged that mare all down the dock, he did. She was rearing up, and Dick would have kept going for ever if Albert hadn't stopped him.

'I will never forget that. It really was something to see, particularly for a little lad like me.

'Dean's didn't hold the young man to the bet afterwards. If they had taken the mare off him it would have put him out of

Tetley horses at work

business. He was just told to keep his big mouth shut in future.'

Albert left school at the age of fourteen and worked for his father at first, but he didn't take the business over when the time came and got a job with a haulage contractor—driving motor lorries. The horse was in decline, vast queues forming outside the knacker's yard, and the lure of the engine was very strong for young men at the time.

'It was a changing world and I will admit that motors were calling me. Everybody wanted to be a motor driver. I might never have come back to horses if I hadn't gone to work for Tetley's more than twenty years ago. I took one of the first articulated lorries that Tetley's bought and drove it for about three years. But one or two of the men looking after the Shires knew me from the old days and it wasn't long before the head horseman called me in, said he had heard I could handle a horse,

97

and would I take out a waggon for him. So I did once or twice, but it didn't pay to go with the horses. The wage in the stables was just over six pound a week, and I was getting eight driving a lorry. Two quid was a lot of money in those days. Eventually, the head horseman asked me if I would like to work full time with the Shires. I'd been to a few shows with him and I do confess I'd got the itch to go back to horses again. There's no finer sight than a good working horse when you ask him to give of his best. Anybody can drive waggons, but there is nothing to compare with being out with a pair of big Shires, watching the world go by with your pipe going and the wind in your hair. It meant taking a drop in money, but I talked it over with the wife and she realized it was inevitable.'

Albert joined a remarkable team of men, among them the last survivors of the old horse generation who rejoiced in names like Black Jack Lazenby, Caruso Robinson and Darkie Burroughs, and moved over for no man, particularly tram-drivers. They chewed tobacco, drank hard and could recall the days before the First World War when wages were low and Tetley's had ninety-eight Shires. Albert still has a note sent to management by a foreman complaining about a man called Ryan who came in to work overtime at the stables on a Sunday ... 'and was paid the same rate as the other men but says he is not coming again for one shilling and threepence. Besides, Mr. Ryan uses bad language at the front office when they pay him ...'

Albert clearly misses the company of men such as these, and laments about the disappearance of the old challenges.

'We are only playing at it today. You just don't see horses going out in three or four feet of snow and laying into their collars with everything they had, a ton of bone, sinew and muscle straining to get several tons on the move. What a stirring moment that was. I often look at the old photographs of the horses we used to have here and I think we'll never see their like again. Why, even ten years ago when I was delivering beer we did three loads a day. And I'm not talking about two or three barrels—we averaged three tons a load, five days a week; and often when we had finished delivering we would be told to wash down the horses because they were going to a Carnival the following day.

'We don't do that sort of hard slog now.'

Tetley's horses are in constant demand all over Yorkshire and beyond to display their ponderous grace at shows and fêtes, and there has been a request to put on a pulling competition matching a Shire against a tug-of-war team, which is becoming a popular activity in the United States. But Albert has turned it down, because his horses are trained to stop when they feel the brake being put on the waggon. Naturally, they would associate the hauling of a tug-of-war team with the brake and wouldn't compete. Anyway, Albert says he does not intend to risk the good name of his company that way.

Nevertheless, he was unable to resist the temptation of a private match six years ago. It happened behind the old stables, which are now being redeveloped.

'I had a good horse, an eighteen-hand gelding called King. He was a half shiverer, which meant it was very difficult to make it back up. So I got fourteen Irish navvies who were working nearby demolishing old buildings, and they all got on a rope. Now King was the type of horse that would give of his best at all times; he wouldn't stop when he was told to go. It was on hard ground and the navvies were wearing their big boots, but when they took the strain he shifted 'em. He was almost laid down, but he shifted 'em!'

If Albert appears to be more enthusiastic about working horses than showing them, it may partly have something to do with a couple of unfortunate experiences in the show-ring. In one he was rather badly injured, and in the other his pride was seriously wounded—which to a true Yorkshireman is almost worse than physical damage.

When he was much younger and not quite the complete horseman he is now, Albert was showing two fine Shires to a set of judges, and men don't come any sterner than heavy horse judges. He thought he was doing well and the crowd was appreciative so as he passed the judges for the second time he called out, 'Would you like me to make them trot?'

There was a frozen silence for a moment as young Albert's words echoed round the ring. Then the senior judge stepped forward and stentoriously delivered himself of this pronouncement:

'Young man! God meant Shire horses to walk. If we had wanted to see trotters, we would have sent for some milk ponies!'

Albert still flinches when he talks about that crushing moment. Oddly, he laughs about the other incident, which would have finished most men with horses for ever.

'Well, everybody laughed at the time. It was at Todmorden Show and me and my old boss, Stanley Stockhill, took a team of Tetley horses. I'd been having a fine time taking the mickey out of an old pal of mine called Pat Flood, who was head horse-

99

man at Thwaites brewery in Blackburn. He had broken his ankle and was wearing a big plaster boot. Then I thought I would have a bit of fun with the guvnor who was taking a small horse called Toby round the ring in the horse in hand class. He used to be quite a joker himself, particularly if he was behind you when you were leading a horse. He would gee it up and you would get swung about a bit. So I thought, right lad, my chance has come to give you one back. I had a rug in my hand so I moved in to give Toby a crack—but he was a quick mover, that horse. I saw it coming but I couldn't do anything about it. I was just that six inches too close, and he kicked me in the stomach. By hell, what a belt—and didn't they laugh, as they picked me up. Even the doctor laughed when he examined me— I was black from the waist downwards.

'Another half inch lower, lad, and you would have been put out of commission altogether," was what he said.

'But I finished up in hospital for ten days with an umbilical hernia. First time I'd ever been ill in my life, not that it was the horse's fault. He never did anything wrong from that day onwards—it was a case of familiarity breeding contempt.'

Albert Hobson took over command of Tetley's stables seven years ago and energetically supervises his eight men—including two blacksmiths—and his amiable Shires, which have now become the symbol of Tetley's presence in the very heart of Yorkshire's major city.

Like most of his brethren, the élite of the heavy horse Freemasonry, he is clearly a totally fulfilled man.

10

A Competitive Man

Harry Ranson knew exactly what he wanted out of life the day he left school at the age of fourteen. He had to wait thirty years before his ambition was realized—and it turned out to be three decades of unremittingly hard labour—but he, too, is a completely contented man today.

He presides over what must be a unique little empire. To go there as dawn breaks is a revelation—the air is full of the strident sound of geese and preening peacocks, forty Muscovy ducks parade around, side by side with flocks of gamecocks and their progeny and guinea fowl. Dominating the scene is a looming black Shire gelding of eighteen hands and more with bright white legs—one of the biggest horses in the land and as handsome as he is huge. A totally rural situation—which thrives, amazingly, just a short haul from the very heart of London.

Harry is the head horseman for Young & Co.'s Brewery, which is situated in Wandsworth High Street, London, a prosperous independent organization which numbers itself among the vitally important few—as far as the survival of the breed was concerned—which never stopped working with heavy horses. Today, they have twenty Shires, only five fewer than the number they owned in 1936. Since the brewery was founded in 1675, that means they can boast an unbroken association with the horse stretching over three centuries.

Harry's patch, which is less than half an acre, runs along the side of the brewery and is separated from the roar of the London traffic by a high wall. He rises every morning at 4.30 and person-

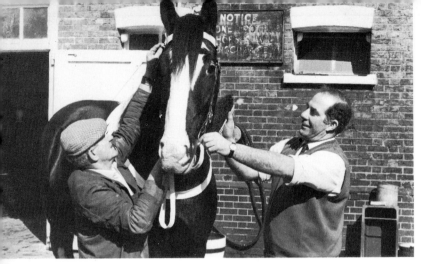

Wandle Ken, then eight years old and weighing over a ton, one of Young's Brewery's champion Shire horses, being prepared for the Heavy Horse Show at Peterborough. Left is Ernie Critchfield, Young's veteran show-driver and right, Harry Ranson, Young's head horse-keeper

Four of Young's magnificent Shires

Mr J. Cornish, the first head horseman at Young's

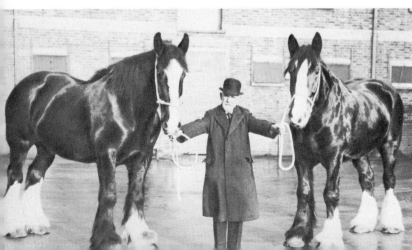

ally feeds every one of his Shires, which means he has been working two hours before most of his eighteen horsemen arrive. Five teams of two are sent out each day to deliver to pubs within a three-mile radius of the brewery and average a total weight of ten thousand tons of beer a year. In the loading yard is a prominently displayed notice warning that any driver trotting a horse will be instantly dismissed, for Harry agrees that God meant Shires to walk.

Harry must have one of the most difficult jobs of any in the heavy horse world because he has to select and train Shires which are capable both of winning prizes regularly at all the top shows, and coping with the ordeal of threading through the London traffic. He rides the continued crises with an aggressive pride. A gravel-voiced man with the barrel-chested physique of a blacksmith (which he once was), he is by nature a competitive person. He clearly looks upon the brewery's motor waggons as his natural enemy and, unlike his counterpart at Tetley's, keeps detailed records to prove to the management that his horses are delivering beer cheaper than mechanized transport.

As he says: 'This is my prime object. The more my directors realize that lorries mean higher and higher expenditure, the longer we shall keep horses and the safer my job and the jobs of my men will be.

'I am as economical as I possibly can be. My annual feed bills are running at about £7,500 a year, and last year it worked out at £5.48 per horse per week. For bedding we used to use nothing but peat moss. Now I put down sawdust and chippings which I get mostly for nothing by clearing out three woodyards. If you include the time taken by my under-foreman and the time of a lorry driver—we also give the people in the yards a dozen pints of beer a week—that brings the cost up to £6.25.

'Which means I can deliver a barrel of beer to a pub at an average of nine pence, which undercuts the motor lorry by about 25 per cent.'

Nor does Harry believe in paying high prices for new horses. He regards today's inflated figures, which value a good gelding at £1500 and upwards, as absolutely ridiculous. On a tour of his immaculate, century-old stables, which seem to bulge at the seams with as fine a team of Shires as you will find anywhere, he reels off names and backgrounds and the prices he paid.

'That's Samson. He was a bag of bones when I bought him down in Truro a year ago, but look at him now. It's a long time since I have seen such power in the second thighs—there must be a good ten-and-a-half inches of bone, and he's not four yet.

Young's
horses o
display

Brigadier, Hercules ... and that is Smiler. I bought him out of a knacker's yard as a four-year-old, and he started to smile as soon as he saw me walk up to him as though he knew he had got a reprieve. Paid £200 for him, same price for that one, £325 for him, £210 for him—but I had to go up to £500 for that one over there.

'However, any good gelding which you can put into a brewer's dray to be driven safely by anybody must be reckoned at a thousand pounds. Their temperament alone is worth three or four hundred.'

Nearly all Young's Shires are black with white legs, the trademark of their stable. And all their names are prefixed with the title Wandle, after the river which runs through Wandsworth. There are some enormous beasts among them and the editors of the *Guinness Book of Records* regularly check with Harry when they seek the identity of the tallest horse in Britain. Young's had the distinction of owning the record holder until just over three years ago. He was a giant of 18.3 hands called Wandle Robert, but tragically he died under anaesthetic after a nail drove through his foot and penetrated his flexible tendon.

Today, the pride of the stable is Wandle Henry Cooper, a potential young champion so called because the Chairman of the Board lunched with the immensely-popular heavyweight boxer on the day they decided to name him. It's an awe-inspiring experience to be present when Henry Cooper is having a work-out on the lunge-rein around the scrap of earth Harry uses for an exercise area. The ground trembles as he hammers it with his soup-plate sized hooves, and every time his bulk passes by it blots out the light.

Amazingly, Harry and his men can exercise a four-horse team in this area, which must make it very crowded, indeed. But when they need to put an eight-horse team through its paces it means a journey to Battersea Park.

Harry is continually searching for equine goliaths but prefers to acquire horses young and just over seventeen hands, so that he can apply his own methods of feeding and training to bring them into the eighteen-hand plus category. The quantity of food a horse like Henry Cooper can shift is staggering. Each and every day he eats ten pounds of bran, ten pounds of brewer's grains, thirty pounds of chaff and just under half a pint of cod liver oil during the winter. But no corn—Harry does not believe in it.

'I think corn is trouble. It overheats horses, they get too excited and silly and that's no good to a man who has to take

Young's brewery yard in
Wandsworth

them out into the streets of London and do a day's work.'

Temperament is more important than either conformation or size for a brewery horse, and Harry has become something of an equestrian psychiatrist in trying to sort out the nervous systems of his charges. He aims to get up to nine years' good service out of each one. Occasionally, one has the strength and equanimity to keep going happily until an advanced age—some years ago a Shire called Wandle Steve celebrated his twenty-first birthday in Young's stables and a brass band was hired to play for him—but others cannot stand the stress.

'Horses are very much like human beings. Give one man a really responsible job and he is dead within two years. Another will relish it and carry on for a lifetime. Some horses you put into the streets around here and they will cope with distractions like double-decker buses without a flicker. But the odd one will never get used to them, stay frightened and refuse to move his

bowels in the street. If you cannot straighten him out he will become a very old horse and three parts finished very quickly. We've been very lucky, but at the moment we do have one called Harold which has not really settled. He worries himself and cannot keep flesh on him—does not look anywhere near as good as the others. I'm hoping he will wear himself into going steady.'

Harry Ranson's consistent success with both show and working horses—ten of his Shires are kept almost exclusively for shows—lends support to the belief so vigorously held by Albert Hobson of Tetley's brewery that the best horsemen come from the towns and cities. For Harry is the ultimate 'townie', a true Cockney born in King's Cross in 1922, the son of a horseman and the grandson of a London hansom cab owner, who worked round Victorian London for a living. Fittingly, it was during the year of Harry's birth that Young and Co. decided to compete in shows so they took on a very experienced man called Charlie Butler from Forshaws in Lincolnshire, the biggest heavy horse stud in the world, for a trial period. Charlie stayed with Young's for forty-two years and he says his appointment was never confirmed.

'A little later he took on my father to help him. It was all arranged for me to join Young's, too, as soon as I left school in 1935. I was to start as an apprentice blacksmith, but when I turned up the manager at the time said the blacksmith did not have enough work to do himself, and I was not hired. So my father got in touch with a pal of his called Jack Plant who was a stud groom at Balderston's at Frithville, the other big Shire stud in Lincolnshire. They had sixty stallions. I went there for a wage of twelve shillings and sixpence a week, all found, and before I made fifteen I was leading a stallion from farm to farm serving mares. At first a stud groom would cycle to the appointments to supervise the covering, but after a bit of training they let me handle the job on my own. It was hard work—and long hours—and I was averaging a hundred miles a week on foot with stallions. I never seemed to stop walking because even in the winter we had to walk a mile there and a mile back to the exercise ground; and I had to take nine stallions a day.

'You had to be careful with some of them stallions. There was one called Masterpiece I remember well. He was so bad tempered you could never let him out after the season finished, so he was put into a paddock every morning. After an hour or so, you had to go in and get him which was a risky business. He would start walking round you with one ear laid back and

Wandle Steve's twenty-first
birthday celebrated with
music in 1966

then have a go at you. He was a vicious pig, that one. When
you went to put his collar on in the box he was just as nasty.
I am not exaggerating when I say he sometimes got his teeth
into my clothes and lifted me clean off the ground.

'Of course, you could never put two stallions together. They
would fight to the death. Before I went to Balderston's one
employee had unfortunately been killed. A horse reared up and
brought his front feet down on the man's head. That sort of
thing can always happen with stallions if you are not careful.
The horse need not necessarily be vicious, just playful.

'I lived with Jack Plant and his wife and they treated me very
well. The food took a bit of getting used to, but in the end I
loved it. They used to kill a forty-stone pig every year, splay
it across a trestle and stuff it with parsley. The fat on its back
would be six inches deep and for lunch on the road I used to
be given two large slices of bread and an inch-thick slice of
home-cured Lincolnshire fat bacon as big as my hand. You had
to cut it up with a knife, but my mouth still waters today when
I think about it.'

For nearly five years Harry pounded the lanes of eastern England in the service of Balderston's and he did it with deformed
feet. He admits they ached a bit, but when he eagerly presented
himself for war service at the age of eighteen he was turned
away, graded three. He ended up on a hospital operating table

108

and did not walk again for a full year. They found his right leg muscle was at least three-quarters of an inch bigger than his left and his right foot a size larger. He also had hammer toes.

'They reckoned I must have had a touch of polio as a child so they broke all my toes and joined them together, and cut into the back of my ankles to lower the arches. When I recovered I had another go at getting into the army, but they still would not have me.'

But one long-held ambition was satisfied during this painful period in Harry's life. He was able to join Young's. His father had left their employ to become a war reserve policeman but Charlie Butler was head horseman and Harry got the job he so badly wanted when he left school—in the blacksmith's shop. For more than three years he hammered away on the anvil, shoeing horses and doing any other job that came along. Although he did not go away to war, he saw plenty of hair-raising action.

'Throughout the London blitz—for more than three years— Charlie Butler and me lived in a loose box next to the horses.

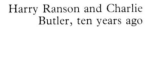

Harry Ranson and Charlie Butler, ten years ago

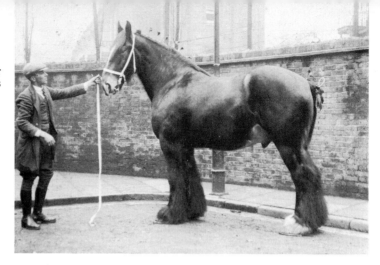

The young Charlie Butler with one of his Shires

His wife and children had been evacuated to Bedford. Sometimes we did not have time to take off our clothes for a whole week, because it was pretty rough round here. One night in 1943 fourteen incendiary bombs dropped on the stable and we had a bit of running around to do to get 'em all out. Another night the hop loft was set alight and then a bomb dropped on the top right hand side of the brewery and the cask shed was demolished. Then they hit the pub on the corner, killing three people. The horses came through it without harm, but they did have a fright one night when a really big one—they said it was an aerial torpedo—dropped three hundred yards away. I think that crater held the record for the Metropolitan area—it was about sixty-five feet wide and thirty feet deep.'

A famous champion gelding, owned by Young's in the 1930s

Wandle Robert, who at 18.3 hands was the tallest horse in England, being led by stable-lad David Hobbs in the Easter Monday Cart Horse Parade at Regents Park

During this harrowing time, a great friendship was forged between Charlie Butler and Harry, which grew into a legendary partnership in the horse world when shows began to be organized again after the war ended. They specialized in the four-horse team events; Charlie trained and got the Shires fit, and Harry drove. From 1946 until 1951 they never lost a class of any kind, and they were entering up to thirty shows a season ending with the Horse of the Year show in October. During this time, Harry was judged by many experts to be the best four-horse team driver in the country, and possibly the world. The awards he collected for four-horse and other classes must weigh half a ton.

Their determination to preserve their unbeaten record during their unrivalled five years of glory was, on one significant occasion almost unbelievable.

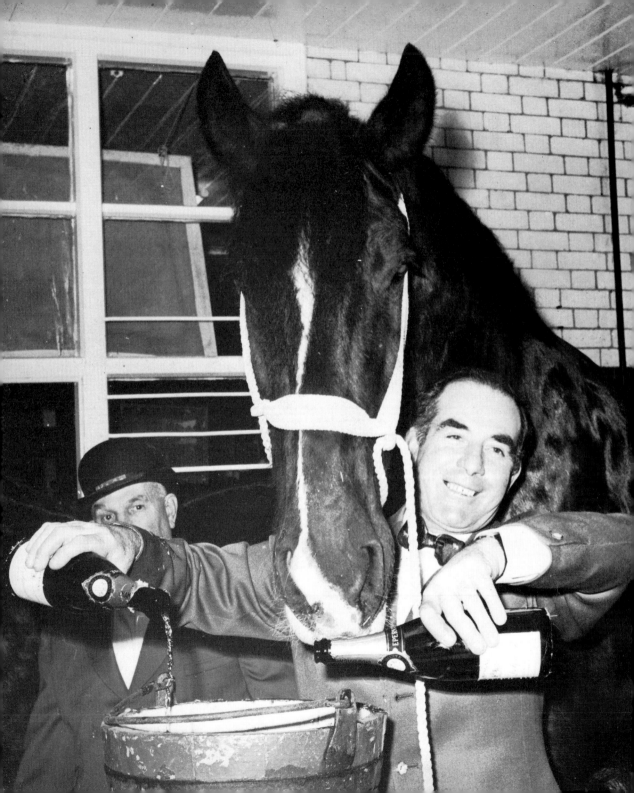

'It happened in 1950 at the Lincolnshire Show at Louth. We had a very good horse at the time called Wandle Jock, but in the single harness event we were up against a man called Frank Starling of Littleport, Cambridge, who is, sadly, dead now. He had been trying to beat us for years and that day brought a hell of a good black horse with three white legs which was so fit that it looked as though he was going to put down old Jock, because we got into a proper mess just before we were due in the show-ring.

'We always had a set routine. Before the horse was put in the shafts, the vehicle was made ready—my dickey seat and strap adjusted, my whip put in position. But this day they did everything but put my whip in position, so one of our men climbed up with the whip and the horse thought it was me. He was very, very fit and got all lit up and excited. I was washing my hands and about to put on my bowler hat when I saw what was happening and ran across and persuaded Jock to hold steady. But when I finally got a grip on the reins he was still tense. He came back and then plunged forward, the veins standing out on his neck because he wanted to get going so badly. He had never acted like that before. Just before we entered the ring we were stopped again, and out there before the judges Frank Starling was walking his horse just nicely. When we set off again, this horse reared up on its hind legs and as we entered the ring we were stopped for a third time! And when I asked him to go again he was so eager he broke the tug chain, which was nearly half an inch in diameter and went from his collar to the shaft. This should have meant we could not go on with the competition and Frank Starling had to win it. But Charlie refused to be beat. He asked me for a handkerchief, so I handed mine down whilst I talked to the horse to keep him steady. He took his own out, went and borrowed one from Frank Starling, who was a real gentleman, and rolled the three handkerchieves together. Then he tied up the two broken links of the chain and off we went with Charlie covering the handkerchieves with his fist—and we won!'

In 1965, Charlie Butler retired and Harry Ranson stepped into the job he had coveted for thirty years. Clearly, he thinks it was worth the wait and relishes every moment he spends among his truly magnificent Shires. Five years after taking over he was awarded the British Empire Medal, which meant the achievement of a most unusual family double because his brother won exactly the same distinction for bravery as a London fire brigade officer.

113

Harry Ranson, best four-in-
hand driver in Britain

Harry is too modest to go into the reasons for this honour, but it no doubt had partly to do with his work for handicapped children. Nor is his outstanding work among heavy horses unknown to the Queen, who first met him to hand over an award before she married. Harry is still raking in the major prizes at shows.

The man he succeeded can also boast a most unusual honour. When he retired, Young and Co. named one of their pubs after him—the Charlie Butler in Mortlake. Maybe the two men will be able to meet one day in the future to talk over their past triumphs, and indulge in a unique conversational opening gambit:

'Where shall we go—your pub, or mine!'

11

The Cock of Westhoughton

According to the *Guinness Book of Records*, the tallest horse in Britain is a celebrated Shire stallion named 'Ladbrook Invader', owned by Mr Arthur Lewis of Tamworth in Staffordshire. He stands nineteen hands one-and-a-half, which means he measures six feet five-and-a-half inches to the withers, or shoulders. But there is a comparatively unknown horse working in an urban area of Lancashire called Majestic which is a mere one-and-three-quarter inches smaller.

He belongs to Jim Walker of Hart Common Farm in Westhoughton, a descendant of a legendary family in those parts, which for generations has always been associated with strength and power—either personally, or in the animals around them. Jim traces his line back to a Robert Walker, one of three brothers who came down across the border from Scotland to seek their fortune. They walked all the way. When they arrived in Lancashire they decided that was far enough. Peter went to Warrington and started Walker's Brewery, William settled in Bolton and founded Walker's Tannery and Robert set up as a farmer in Westhoughton.

All three enterprises still flourish—the brewery and the farm are still run by Walkers. The old family names of Peter, Roger and Robert are still given to male heirs and Jim was staggered during a visit last year to Walker's brewery when he saw a painting of the original Peter Walker. He says it was the image of his father's younger brother—also called Peter.

There is another direct link with the past in Jim's branch

of the family—heavy horses. To this day, the farming Walkers have always bred, traded and worked their land with them, and are now the only people in the area who do. Jim has a weakness for really big Shires, although some other enthusiasts scorn them because they believe them too ponderous for steady work. Jim says he has proved this theory false, owns other Shires only slightly smaller than Majestic and clearly is proud to be the owner of the most powerful animal in the district. He is, in-directly, following another family tradition because his great-uncle Dick, who before the turn of the century had a farm in Dickinson Lane, was for years the Cock of Westhoughton. That meant he was the best fighter in the town, in the days when it was a fiercely-contested honour. Great-uncle Dick founded his reputation in the most spectacular way and Jim remembers the story in detail, as told by his father.

'In Dick's time, there were a lot of farmers in market garden-ing in the Ormskirk area who used to set off for Bolton Market on the midnight before market day, with their produce on a horse-drawn cart. They would walk by the side of their horses all the way and arrive early in the morning. When they had sold their stuff they would always have a drop to drink before all setting off back together.

'Now Dickinson Lane where my Great-uncle had his place was a very bad, narrow and winding road and one day he was going down it with a load on his cart when he met seven of these chaps all going back home in a line with their empty carts. One of them was three parts drunk and bumped into Dick's wheel as he went by. Now Dick had a fiery temper and, not at all bothered by the odds, demanded an explanation from the man. Inevitably, a fight started and Dick knocked him into the ditch. The next man went for Dick and he finished up in the ditch too. Altogether, he put six of them into the ditch, one after the other. The seventh was waiting his turn, but changed his mind and hurried away.

'Dick was not a tall man, but he was very strong and sturdy and became known throughout the area for his courage. The question of who was the best man around here was traditionally decided at Westhoughton Wakes. There was a hell of a scrap every year at the fair as various people put up to have a go at whoever was Cock. My father said that Great-uncle Dick was Cock of Westhoughton for year after year and in the end they had to find a big navvy to put up against him before he got beat.'

Jim Walker was born in 1914 and was himself an enthusiastic

Jim Walker today   Jim Walker running a grey gelding
Jim at a ploughing match in the 1950s

witness of other feats of muscular prowess—involving horses, not men. He recalls the time when it was quite normal for a Shire to pull two-wheeled cars laden with two tons of bricks on their way to building sites and still speaks in awe of an amazing example of equine strength he saw in the thirties.

'It was on the docks in Liverpool, and I will never forget it. This horse was pulling a four-wheeled waggon laden with twelve tons of B.O.C.M. dairy nuts. Twelve tons! He looked a poor old thing, too, but was he fit. Doing it every day, you see. There used to be some marvellous horse handlers in Liverpool. They had a special knack and always won the weight-pulling contests in London. Getting a big load on the move is the tricky part and they were masters at it. You should never start a four-wheeled vehicle with a dead straight pull when it has a big load on; always give it a slight turn and it will roll a lot easier.

'That's the way they used to go about it. Mind, they were probably the best teamsmen in the country. They were a rough and ready lot those Liverpool men, but they could get the best out of any horse.'

During the days between the wars when the horse was the king of the road, to be a good horseman commanded respect everywhere, despite your social position or personal weaknesses. Jim Walker knew one outstanding example.

'He was called Gerry Oakes, and he knew horses. One of the best around here in his time. He and his brother, Bob, had a farm and were in the hay and straw trade. They used to go to Manchester three or four times a week with loads of fodder; but they drank a lot and one day they were coming back from a trip a bit the worse for wear. Bob was riding on the shaft when he fell off going down a hill and got run over and killed. Gerry carried on alone for a while but he eventually went broke and finished up working for the Co-op, and sleeping in the stall next to the Co-op butcher's pony. He did that for years. But he was a character, always smoked a cigar and used to go in the Red Lion at dinner-time for a drop of whisky. Everyone who knew him respected him, and when he died in 1939 even the police walked with the cortège. I took him to the church myself on a lorry with two horses—I did the same for my father—and the local hay and straw dealer did not send a usual wreath. He went to the trouble of making up a little stack of hay and thatched it.

'There was another character who lived in Bolton called Jack Worthington, who was also a very good judge of a horse like

Mrs Kathleen Walker

Jim Walker driving Majestic
and Major

Gerry Oakes. They both used to help people pick one out. Old Jack used to work for a local vet and one day a woman came in with two dogs complaining that they would not eat. Well, these dogs were so fat and under-exercised that they could scarcely walk, so Jack told the woman he would get the vet to look after them and put them in a little pen in the loft. A week later she came back, and as she walked in Jack realized he had forgotten all about them. He had put down plenty of water, but no solid food. He dashed up to the loft and there they were, bouncing about and very glad to see him. The woman was delighted—she thought he had worked a wonderful cure!'

Jim is clearly a traditionalist who regrets the passing of the colourful and charismatic days of his youth. He started winning medals for his Shires way back in 1936 and even resisted the lure of the motor car until the 1940s, preferring instead to use a hackney and trap. But he refused to follow the trend on every other farm, kept on breeding and working heavy horses, and over the years has seen his stock sink in value to almost nothing and then swing back to today's soaring prices.

Jim's preference for giants among horses make his stables an alarming place for the novice to visit, although they are extremely placid animals. He has twelve Shires altogether, including two stallions and four mares, and he can almost match Majestic with another massive gelding which measures eighteen hands two. When he bought him he was called Humphrey, but as Jim says—'How can you sit up there and shout "Geddup, Humphrey"—you would look a right ninny.' So Humphrey now has the more suitable name of Captain, and when he and Majestic take to the road together in harness it is truly a sight to behold.

Nevertheless Jim does admit that the finest working horse he owned was a modest beast of not much over sixteen hands, and a crossbred to boot. He was a gelding called Tommy, dark brown with three white feet.

'And he wasn't just the best I ever had—he was the best I have ever seen. He started out as the daftest thing that ever lived. I first saw him at Preston Auction Mart where he was so wild he cleared the ring out and then reared up and put his front feet on the auctioneer's rostrum. But even then there was something about him I liked. I bid sixty-five quid for him, but the owner had paid seventy-eight guineas for him in Wales. He did curse me, and there was no sale. A few weeks later the same horse came up at a Manchester auction and went wild again.

Jim drives a Victorian horse bus in Manchester

Eventually his owner turned up at my farm one night during haytime and asked if I had a horse that could mow. It happened I had—a big but quiet Irish cross which I had bought for forty-five pounds. So this chap swapped Tommy for him and gave me twenty-five quid into the bargain.

'First thing I did with Tommy was harness him to a hay-shaker and he acted like a lunatic—dragged me all over the place. Then I tried him in the mowing machine and the same thing happened, so I just turned him out and let him run about until the autumn. But I still had faith in him; I put him to ploughing in the winter and after two or three weeks he became a wonderful horse and ploughed every day throughout the season. He could be a problem even then, particularly when cutting corn which sent him potty again. But I found a way of curing him of that—tied one of his front legs up and made him go on three legs for part way round the field. He would be all right then, but each time he came fresh to a job involving machinery that clanked and vibrated I had to repeat the discipline. I do not believe in beating horses. Sometimes you have to give them one good hiding and be done with it. But to keep on hammering at them is no use; it just turns them stubborn.

'I worked Tommy for a few years until 1950—much longer than I normally hang on to geldings—but one local man kept pestering me to sell him. He had a mare I wanted, worth about seventy pounds, so we did a straight swap, but I only agreed on condition that if he ever wanted to part with him I would have first option. Straight away, the new owner decided to take Tommy to the blacksmith, put him in a milk float and set off. It was a right turn into the road towards the smithy, but Tommy had other ideas, turned left and kept going for three or four miles before this chap managed to stop him.

'The day after he came back with Tommy and asked me to swap him for a cow, which had cost me nineteen pounds, and gave me six quid as well. So you could say I did well with Tommy in more ways than one because that deal meant he stood me at nothing.

'What a horse he was. He never refused a job and never stopped. I would have to change the horse working with him, but never Tommy. You could keep him going all day and he would come back home at night stepping out as though he was walking on springs and fresh out of the stable. He was a master at drilling—I did not even put the reins on him, just controlled him by voice only; and I usually put new horses with him when I was breaking them in because if they misbehaved he would

Jim driving an antique cart with Peter and Pilot

Masterpiece, Jim's stallion   Jim and Majestic

turn his head round and give them such a nip on the nose. It certainly quietened them down.'

Tommy's extraordinary intelligence and ability probably saved his own life and that of a gelding called Captain, working in harness with him at the time, when they fell foul of an unusual hazard on Jim Walker's 120-acre farm. It runs between two of his fields, a narrow two hundred yard long ditch which falls to a depth of twelve feet in places. Called the scutch by some locals, a stream runs along the bottom and trees and bushes grow along the edge. Several of Jim's horses have fallen down it over the years and if they dropped in an awkward position they usually did not survive the experience. One had been rubbing on the wire fence which runs along one side of the ditch, broke a post and tumbled over and hung there with one leg caught in the wire; another tried grazing too far down the bank and slipped in to end up with her feet higher than her body; a third became trapped by her hips under a low branch of a tree.

Getting the horses out posed major problems. One mare was still alive when Jim found her one night and he called for help from a group of soldiers under canvas nearby—the incident happened during the last war. They brought a searchlight and it took a full hour for fifteen servicemen, every available neighbour and a tractor to bring the horse out—and she died the next day.

Tommy and Captain were ploughing by the ditch one day when the man handling them went too close to the edge. The banking collapsed under the weight and the whole lot went in, horses and plough. Jim still glows with pride when recalling the way his favourite horse handled the situation.

'Not only did he get himself out, he pulled Captain out, too—and then the plough. No doubt about it—I have never known his equal and I have seen a few in my time.'

Tragically, Tommy died during the fifties at the comparatively early age of ten, and the memory of the way he went, game to the last, can still visibly upset both Jim and his wife.

'I think he strained his heart. Gave that bit too much, which was typical of him. We were getting in potatoes and the going was very heavy, very bad. He did not collapse or anything like that but he started going downhill straight after—sweated a lot and lay down a lot; then he just died.

'It was heartbreaking.'

12

Steam, Wind and Horses

If there is one characteristic shared by all farms which have steadfastly used heavy horses come what may, it is a sense of timelessness. They look, smell and sound like farms should look, smell and sound and are far removed from the proliferating agricultural factories where the nose is assaulted by the latest wonder chemical and the ears ring with the incessant whine of machinery.

Some may dismiss this view as pure romanticism and totally impractical, but the traditional farms do seem to prosper equally as well and the men who run them are certainly more at peace with themselves and their environment. Geoff Morton's spread at Holme-on-Spalding Moor in Yorkshire must be an outstanding example as he moves towards 1980 with much the same measured tread with which he met the challenges of the sixties.

There is a perpetual cycle at Hasholme Carr Farm which pivots comfortably on his horses, and all Geoff wants to do is improve it—which he accepts must be a very gradual process. Self-sufficiency is his aim so that his farm and family are insulated as much as possible from the vagaries of the outside world. Geoff can even calmly turn hazards into an advantage. Along the lower parts of his farm there must have been a thick wood some thousands of years ago which was flattened by the strong south-westerly winds, and swallowed up in the peaty soil. This means the land is studded with bog oak, which his plough sometimes hits with disastrous results.

Whenever this happens, Geoff and his sons dig round the ancient, petrified lumps, chain them to one or more of the horses and haul them out; then they are left to dry out for a year.

'It's a very useful source of fuel for us, keeps us warm all winter long; and with the amount of bog oak on my land we won't have to worry about coal or central heating for quite a few years.'

The only significant change on Geoff's farm in more than a decade happened in the spring of 1977, when, after much deliberation, he went to France with Charles Pinney to help him find an Ardennes stallion, and came back with two four-year-old roan mares for himself. That increased his population of heavy horses to twenty-eight because one of the newcomers, called Hilda, produced a filly foal (much to Geoff's delight) within two weeks of her arrival; the other, Hallette, was also in foal.

'This does not mean I am switching out of Shires. I just feel the Ardennes have a useful part to play on my farm; they are very hardy, economical and docile and absolutely ideal for beginners.'

Obviously Geoff sees commercial opportunities in the Ardennes breed. He has no doubt that the number of people wanting to start working their land with heavy horses is growing steadily, and he does breed to sell. During the year before his investment in the Ardennes mares he placed four Shires on the market. He now has an informal partnership with Charles Pinney, who brought his stallion to Holme-on-Spalding Moor immediately after Hilda had foaled so that she could be covered again at the crucial time.

Imposant Du Bourbeau—known as Bill to his friends—is almost certainly the only Ardennes stallion in Britain and he is a beast of much distinction. Last year he was judged to be the breed champion. Charles paid more than a thousand pounds for him but is convinced he has a remarkable bargain.

'You see, the French are so keen to see the breed properly established in Britain—but I don't think they will be so generous again, and I must say I have been absolutely staggered by him. Within a week he was broken and working with a mare he had just served. Then I put him in a reversible plough, a difficult machine, and he coped with no bother. I also drilled twenty acres with him. And the day after he served Geoff's mare he was working with a mare he had never seen before. He should have gone loopy, but he didn't. A quite exceptional horse.'

Charles also brought across another mare, a three-year-old

Geoff Morton with
his Ardennes mares
at Holme-on-
Spalding Moor

called Ironie, which put his total up to three. All are in foal to Bill. In 1978 he will put Bill's services on the market. He says it will improve British stock of any kind, putting in substance and bone, and hopefully, the renowned Ardennes temperament. For a young man, Charles has made a sizeable investment in the French breed but is confident that it will return a steady dividend.

As for Geoff Morton, the proportion of his income derived from horses increases all the time. He has got out of pigs, has not replaced them with cattle and in recent seasons has used his arable land for growing grains and potatoes. The fame that comes with constant exposure on the media brings in a steady stream of quite profitable jobs, displaying his horses at various events around the north. Twice a year he holds an Open Day at his farm, with all his horses harnessed up and demonstrating their ability around his spread, the local farrier at work in the yard and a magnificent steam engine thundering away at corn threshing.

Up to three thousand people turn up and pay admission at his farm-gate! Just the kind of thing to inflame the ambitions of most men, but Geoff appears to have little regard for such temporary phenomena. And he is, no doubt, right to be dismissive. There are much more important things in life than a public image and he knows it better than most.

'I am a reasonably satisfied man. I do have the odd grumble about the weather or the crops but it's a happy kind of life here. Ambitions? Well, not really. Not the sort of thing you could dignify with the title of ambition. Other men yearn to own the Horse of the Year or win the Champion Stallion award at Peterborough—but not me. If I have one small desire, it might be to visit the United States and see them work with the big teams over there.'

If he did, the perfect way for Geoff to go would be by windjammer across the Atlantic and by steam car to America's grain belt. For as he says—and there can be no more fitting conclusion to this book:

'I have often felt that a combination of horses and steam and wind gives you all the power you need for anything that is really worth doing.'